THE CHARTER SCHOOLS DECADE

Anne Turnbaugh Lockwood

SCARECROWEDUCATION
Lanham, Maryland • Toronto • Oxford
2004

Published in the United States of America
by ScarecrowEducation
An imprint of The Rowman & Littlefield Publishing Group, Inc.
4501 Forbes Boulevard, Suite 200, Lanham, Maryland 20706
www.scarecroweducation.com

PO Box 317
Oxford
OX2 9RU, UK

British Library Cataloguing in Publication Information Available

Library of Congress Cataloging-in-Publication Data
Lockwood, Anne Turnbaugh.
  The charter schools decade / Anne Turnbaugh Lockwood.
      p. cm.
  Includes bibliographical references and index.
  ISBN 1-57886-038-5 (pbk. : alk. paper)
  1. Charter schools—United States—History—20th century. I. Title.
LB2806.36 .L63 2004
371.01'0973—dc21

                                            2003014608

♾™ The paper used in this publication meets the minimum requirements of
American National Standard for Information Sciences—Permanence of
Paper for Printed Library Materials, ANSI/NISO Z39.48-1992.
Manufactured in the United States of America.

CONTENTS

ACKNOWLEDGMENTS

Authors always say they owe a "profound debt of gratitude" to certain people when they finish a book. In this case, these familiar words could not ring more true.

This book simply could not have been written without the provocative ideas, constant encouragement, and outright insistence of Joe Schneider, former deputy executive director at the American Association of School Administrators. I am indebted to Joe for his expertise on charter schools—and his marvelous generosity with his wide-ranging knowledge about education in general and the art of writing in particular.

Helen Marks Dicks read this book in a variety of incarnations—ranging from its very first page to first complete draft—and believed.

Laura and Denis Vogel helped enormously in ways they may not even realize and at times that were always right.

My parents, Roy C. and Zora Turnbaugh, who endured the Great Depression and World War II to spend the next forty years working in the public schools, were steadfast in their belief that a fine public education is the path to a better life. They were right.

—Anne Turnbaugh Lockwood, June 2003

INTRODUCTION

Beginning in 1991, when the first charter school opened in Minnesota, the charter schools movement has charmed a diverse group of stakeholders. Its rhetoric was persuasive and strong. It tapped into parental dissatisfaction with their lack of control over the public schools their children attended or planned to attend, and it appealed to state legislators looking for a way to appease these constituents that would not cost additional money.

As the good news about the original Minnesota charter school—soon more than one school—began to spread, parents and other educational consumers began to learn of "independent" public schools. Charter schools burgeoned; enabling legislation was enacted in other states during the flush years of the 1990s. And as charter schools grew, the rhetoric that surrounded them brought together a host of unlikely allies who applauded their expansion and growth.

These allies included homeschoolers, Christian fundamentalists, advocates of school choice, and parents in search of a new alternative to the public education their children were receiving—as well as parents of children who had not yet entered public schools. Huddled under the same tent, these groups and individuals found hope in the charter schools movement, lobbied their state legislators, and advanced their cause to fruition in thirty-nine states in addition to Washington, D.C., and Puerto Rico.

THE CHARTER SCHOOLS ACCOMPLISHMENT EXAMINED

How did something so bold, so sweeping, and so brash gain the cachet that the charter schools movement has achieved? How was it possible that these "independent" public schools managed to grab public monies to fund themselves at the expense of regular public schools? How did they overcome fierce opposition from the education cartel?

It actually is quite an amazing feat that a grassroots effort managed to expand so dramatically—charter schools grew approximately 14 percent in 2002—despite doubts, brickbats, and warnings from think tanks, professional educational associations, and much of the education media.

STRONG SUPPORT, UNLIKELY ALLIES, PREDICTABLE OPPOSITION

The charter schools movement has an enviable advantage over regular public schools: a sturdy, well-balanced foundation of support. Legislators on both sides of the aisle, education-reform advocates, and infusions of federal and private funds, as well as ample helpings of favorable attention from the mainstream media, have lent the movement broad appeal and built positive public relations.

It is no wonder that school leaders find this movement a threat to the usual way they educate students and to the ways in which they have been trained to do so. Rarely do school leaders in the regular public system enjoy the support that charter schools have grown accustomed to. Nor do the rules and regulations with which they must comply permit the same freedoms from conforming to such onerous rules outside the charter schools movement. Instead, regular public schools are held accountable to provisions that charter schools escape. This movement lies outside their practical realm, and quite naturally, they are uncomfortable with it, at minimum, and virulently opposed to it, at maximum.

The opposition of regular public school educators does not lessen the confusion for many educational consumers left bewildered about these "independent" public schools. They may not understand whether charter schools are public or private, how they are led and staffed, who attends them, and why charter schools have come into being in the first place. Who needed these schools, and why were they created? Or perhaps, were they needed at all?

WHY CREATE CHARTER SCHOOLS?

All these questions are worth scrutiny. "Independent" public schools, as charter schools like to call themselves, did not emerge from a vacuum. Instead, these schools were developed because of strongly held beliefs about the right to choose a public school. Parental frustration with regular public schooling and the hope that an alternative to "the usual way of doing business" could help many children succeed in school fueled the cause as well.

Most of the arguments in favor of charter schools push public control of "independent" public schools to the fore. When they do so, they hit the Achilles' heel of many parents—that they cannot exercise much control over what, how, or with whom their children learn. These arguments strike a spot that is almost exquisitely painful: parental feelings of helplessness when they deal with the school their child is forced to attend. Low-income, non-English-speaking, and affluent parents can share the same sentiment, a belief that draws them together and pulls them in the direction of school choice: *The schools do not listen to us, and I want something different (preferably smaller and more personalized) for my child.*

SCHOOL CHOICE ADVOCATES AND
CHARTER SCHOOL SUPPORTERS

But parents are joined by another powerful camp: school choice advocates who may or may not have school-age children. These groups may overlap at times, but advocates of choice see the charter schools movement in terms that are more clearly political. They are convinced that competition and the application of market forces will spur public schools to improve. While they may actually *prefer* vouchers—a much bolder political move through which a student can take a voucher to the school of his or her choice—they realize that charter schools are a more acceptable political compromise. And since charter schools succeed so well in gathering many different people under the same tent, they result in advancing a more politically palatable agenda of school choice (Wells et al. 1998).

The other large group supporting charter schools consists of either parents who are dissatisfied with the experiences their child or children have had with the regular public schools or parents who are seeking more control of their child's education at the outset. These parents see themselves primarily as *consumers* and are not willing to take a backseat to regular public school methods and procedures.

STATE LEGISLATORS BECOME INVOLVED

Both parents and advocates of school choice—who may be one and the same—exert pressure on state legislators to reform the laws to provide for schools of choice, such as charter schools. While vouchers may not be a popular concept in many legislators' home districts, the same legislators can embrace choice and please their constituents by enacting charter schools legislation. They show their constituents that they understand the appeal of smaller schools and more personalized instruction—and they do all this without increased spending by the taxpayer.

State legislators are also quite pleased that charter schools are an inexpensive gesture toward reform and choice, what has been called "reform on the cheap." It does not cost the state more money to enact charter schools; in fact, start-up funds are frequently slightly less than what regular public schools receive.

In passing these laws and applauding new or converted charter schools, legislators are in an enviable position: they have enacted a "reform" that is popular, that gives power to the people, and that is so elusive it is difficult to criticize. Few legislators will lose an election because they have supported charter schools, but championing vouchers is a whole other matter.

But this enviable turn of events is beginning to change as the economy takes a downturn. Legislators, pressed to the wall by severe fiscal cuts for public education, now are forced to reexamine their charter schools legislation—and charter school advocates are beginning to squeal in protest.

STEM-WINDER RHETORIC

One of the key pieces of the charter schools movement has been the stem-winder rhetoric that has been used to advance it. This rhetoric has worked in statehouses, in small parent groups that have gathered with hopeful aspirations, and in the popular media.

At first, though it has since been played down, a central piece of pro-charter rhetoric was the assertion that charter schools could change the regular public school system for the better, simply by their presence and example. Instead of regulating education, charter schools could *deregulate* it—and heightened innovation and student achievement would be only two of the many positive outcomes.

This particular piece of rhetoric, which could be called "the charter schools bargain," caught the fancy of pro-charter education reformers, who used it in many of their speeches. Ultimately, it was not as persuasive as other parts of the charter schools argument, probably because it remained more theoretical and abstract than the simple rhetoric around parental choice of public schools.

Advocates advanced many other arguments, and the fascinating aspect of these contentions is their ever-shifting nature over the past decade. They have remained fluid and adaptable—unlike the arguments *against* charter schools advanced by school leaders in the regular, huge public school system.

For example, one strong claim advocates use—that no one is forced to attend a charter school—still has broad appeal. Other assertions include the link between parental involvement and successful schools, small school/class size and student engagement in their studies, and parental/staff influence over what students learn. Charter school supporters have quickly dropped arguments that are too esoteric for their clients in favor of more popular arguments.

All these stem-winder polemics can be quite persuasive, particularly to a group of parents who clearly want something better for their children than attendance at the regular public school where the parent may be shunted aside. They consider a public education an entitlement, something every American child should receive, and they believe it should be what they consider a *good* public education, not an inferior public education.

REACTION AND RECOILING

But everyone is not so pleased with the development and rapid expansion of charter schools. Understandably, most people in the regular public schools greet the many-sided and constantly shifting arguments of charter school advocates with considerable skepticism and anger. School leaders can hardly be expected to embrace a movement that siphons off funds from their own districts—especially in a time of growing, severe financial hardship for public education. They would like to keep those funds and those students in their districts under traditional guidelines. Also, they cannot be expected to welcome "independent" public schools that challenge the status quo and turn parents from the *recipients* of educational services to the *consumers* of these services.

This shift in power and control lies at the heart of all debates about school choice. It is especially threatening to school leaders who are used to exercising leadership in their own domains. Suddenly turning things around—to a consumer/client relationship in which the education received is the "goods"—smacks too much of business and not enough of public education to these leaders.

THE CYCLE OF DISCONTENT

While advocates debate the benefits of school choice in a theoretical and abstract manner, the issue is immediate and concrete to parents. "Regular" public schools may make it quite clear—fairly or unfairly—to disgruntled parents that their children, in fact, do not fit in. At that point, the cycle of discontent becomes complete. After frequent school visits and complaints, parents risk being tagged by educators as "troublemakers." Teachers and principals may become frustrated with what they view as constant demands. They do not want to deal with parents who haul their problems with the public schools into all sorts of public venues, embarrassing public school staff and administrators.

Whether they are just starting out with a youngster in kindergarten and choose a charter school or whether they feel burned by "the system," charter school parents want schools that are responsive directly to *their* educational visions for *their* children—and they believe that the regular public school "bureaucracy" is the problem. Bureaucracy is a large word that means large things. (It is also a word frequently used in the pro-charter rhetoric.) If they have children who have spent any time in school, their experience has shown failure to get what they want for their children.

Parents who are just starting out with the public schools turn to charter schools with hope—but also with some trepidation about the regular public schools that encourages them to seek an alternative, publicly funded path for their children. Parents whose child has had bad experiences in school turn to charter schools in frustration. When the child has a problem and a response is either inadequate or slow, parental irritation grows. Shunted from staffer to staffer and from department to department, many parents simply do not know what to do. They seek audiences with the principal, the superintendent, and the school board—anyone who will listen.

And their children may not, in fact, fit in well in regular public schools that are geared to the majority. They may be problematic, from the school's point of view, because their behavior is disruptive, because they are non-English-speaking, or because in other ways they fall outside the mainstream. They may be bullied or simply unhappy. At the very least, they may need special attention, and their parents do not believe overwhelmed teachers can provide it.

This does not mean that traditional public schools want to *lose* these students. If they lose them, they lose the funding that accompanies them. Instead, they want them to comply with the rules, structure, and socialization incumbent on all children. And they want their parents to comply: to be more like other parents, like the parents of children without problems. Those parents treat teachers and principals with the respect they believe they deserve as professionals who work with their children.

But if the traditional public schools *do* lose these students, the seldom-discussed truth is that ultimately they gain some peace and quiet. Many irritants are eased when parents, unhappy staff, and problematic students move into charter schools and out of the traditional public schools. And most school staff now realize, although they may be loath to admit it, that charter schools are not a threat. They will not take their best students away—as was originally feared when charter schools began in the early 1990s. It is now much more likely that students who have some sort of need that is not met will enroll in a charter school—if one is available—or seek refuge in the new hybrid of virtual charter schools that is sprouting up in a few states.

Charter schools have become a part of the American landscape in the past decade. It is past time for a ten-year review, an examination of what they have accomplished, where they have failed, where the laws have succeeded or failed, and where this long, expensive educational experiment is headed.

Some definite, interesting shifts on the horizon warrant this scrutiny. State policymakers no longer seem as uncritical of charter schools in the states that permit their existence. Instead, they are using the downturn in the economy as an opportunity to revisit and refine their charter school legislation—usually not to the benefit of the charter school.

Federal legislation, which calls for increased accountability for traditional public schools, also contributes to a new feeling of pressure. In the past, charter school authorizers (those agencies that supervised charter schools) had little oversight responsibility. Their duties were largely symbolic; authorizers were cheerleaders for the rapid growth of charter schools in their states. This has now changed, as *authorizers* turn into *regulators*—a type of "bureaucratic creep" that some in the school choice movement have predicted and dreaded (Finn 2002).

The creativity that parents and other advocates of choice have demonstrated in establishing these schools is an entity that *all* public school educators could emulate. Rather than fight charter schools, they could co-opt them, use them as examples, and even turn to them for inspiration to change the larger system, as the original bargain promised. School leaders might well ask themselves how well their districts really are doing, how they might deal better with "problem" parents, and how not to wince when they see the test scores, particularly in hard-to-staff schools.

1

THE FIRST DECADE OF CHARTER SCHOOLS

The educational establishment has both a profound dislike and a deep distrust of charter schools. But in refusing to acknowledge the powerful sentiments that charter school supporters churn up in their advocacy of school choice, the establishment does itself a disservice. It negates the fact that many Americans are dissatisfied with public schools and seek a different option for their children. It also turns its back on the fact that school districts are capable of creating their own charters, thus annoying their critics and pleasing this constituency.

Traditional educators may be annoyed by charter advocates, but the latter represent the tremendous diversity of the American population: everyone from potential homeschoolers to members of the Christian right to parents of color in urban areas. Some are affluent; others are low income. All, at some level, believe that "traditional" public schools are not the place to send their children for an education.

The educational establishment is motivated more by fear than by any other sentiment. It smells a twin threat that is much greater in traditional educators' fantasies than in reality: the potential of charter schools (1) to siphon off funds from their districts and (2) to skim their top students, leaving regular schools with less money to educate those students left behind. To a large extent, public school educators spit out the words "charter" and "voucher" with the same disgust. But they are not the same threat.

CHARTER SCHOOL PARENTS, STUDENTS, AND PERSONALIZATION

Studies of charter schools find that their student bodies are generally composed of two groups: (1) students who leave the traditional public system out of unhappiness or a "lack of fit" and (2) students who begin their educations in charter schools because their parents believe that the size and the general "tone" of charter schools are better for their child (U.S. Department of Education 2001).

Charter schools are intensely personal. At their core, they are all about families, whether they are traditional two-parent families or whether they are nontraditional families. These families—the sending families—partner with charter school staff in a synergistic way that bonds students to teachers, parents to staff, and parents to other parents. This type of educational intimacy is something else that the educational establishment tends to ignore, simply because it does not fit the way bureaucracies are constructed. Yet it is a type of personalization that has been recommended by education reformers since Sputnik.

Parents of charter school students typically are involved with instructional staff and principals, integrating themselves actively in the life of their children's school. Members of the instructional staff rely on parents to perform a multitude of tasks that range from helping in the classroom to community outreach to significant fund-raising. This family environment tells parents that their child is actually quite "normal," that children have different learning styles, and that the smaller class size typical in charter schools (in addition to the smaller size of charter schools themselves) will help personalize education for their child. In so doing, the problem (and label) vanishes; the child is absorbed as a part of the school culture. This school culture welcomes *them* as well and, in fact, in some cases makes their participation mandatory.

BEYOND PARENTS AND STUDENTS TO SCHOOL CHOICE ADVOCATES

In addition to the simple appeal that charter schools extend to prospective parents, they beckon to a whole segment of the population that looks at education in terms of pulling one lever to enact a certain result. This segment believes in wielding choice and competition as a tool. These individuals—whether they are parents or charter advocates (or both)—have bought into the rhetoric spun by charter school advocates that *charter schools have the ability to change the larger system for the good, merely by their presence and example.*

State legislators have injected themselves into this picture. Currently, forty states (Maryland became the fortieth state in May 2003) in addition to Washington, D.C., and Puerto Rico have charter schools legislation on the books. This legislation is in varying degrees of implementation and will be discussed in much more detail in chapter 3. At its core, the legislation offers more autonomy to charter schools than to regular public schools—in return for increased accountability. At least, this was the bargain. It was a bargain based largely on stem-winder rhetoric, and it never materialized. Although charter advocates try to prove increased accountability in exchange for improved student outcomes, they continue to have difficulty making this case.

A DIFFERENT CLIMATE FOR CHARTER SCHOOLS

While the 1990s saw a warm climate for charter schools, policymakers and parents now confront chillier foes. State policymakers are considering shifts in laws that only two years ago made charter schools seem strong, viable, and unassailable. Now, many wonder if they have gone too far in extending freedoms to these schools.

For example, Ohio has experienced a protracted battle in its legislature. Ohio's five-year charter law was challenged based on its constitutionality (*Education Week*, December 11, 2002) in a suit filed by the Ohio Federation of Teachers, the Ohio School Boards Association, and the state chapter of the PTA.

After constant revisions and rewrites, the final bill imposes a host of new regulations on Ohio charter schools—ranging from "remedial education to Internet filtering" (*Education Week*, December 11, 2002). This major change in Ohio's law was prompted by recommendations that emerged from a state audit that harshly criticized state oversight of charter schools (*Education Week*, December 11, 2002). One of the largest changes relates to who can grant charters (these people or agencies are called "charter authorizers") and adds more bureaucratic provisions to the entire process (the authorization process also will be discussed in more detail in chapter 3).

Indiana, which is one of the newer states to pass charter legislation, now experiences a budget debate over charter schools. The fear that many noncharter, public school administrators have about charter schools—that they will siphon off district funds—is increasing as Indianapolis opens its first charter schools. Why is this the case, when in most states this fear has not been realized? Unlike students in other states, most students in Indianapolis's charter schools previously attended private schools, so educations were not paid for out of public funds but out of parental pockets. Now these students are flooding the charter schools in Indianapolis and are an additional expense. Public funds must be shared with the start-up schools, leaving less money per pupil than if the charters had not been approved.

California, which had a liberal policy that blended home-based programs with on-site charter programs, now sees progressive cuts. In 2001, California charter schools of this type saw a 5 percent cut, followed by a cut in 2002 of 20 percent for students defined as nonclassroom-based, with a projected 30 percent cut for students beginning school in the fall of 2003 (*Education Week*, January 15, 2003).

This is not a situation unique to California. Similar programs have taken deep budget hits across the nation. One major concern among state policymakers in California and elsewhere is the close coalition between homeschoolers (who enroll in a cyber charter school at public expense), the explosion of online learning, and the diversion of public funds to pay for parent- and Internet-provided education. The coalition, some believe, could result in profiteering from online companies eager to provide programs to publicly funded homeschoolers.

Maryland faces an egregious budget program but instead has focused on debates among state policymakers about whether charter teachers should continue as union members and who should authorize charter schools. In fact, the entire issue of charter authorization could undo everything charter school designers sought to try: remove autonomy, increase bureaucratic regulations, increase reporting requirements, and, in short, make charter schools as similar to other public schools as possible.

And in the last two years there has been a new development: cyber charter schools. These schools put students in front of computers, usually at home, to learn online at public expense. This has occasioned lawsuits and anger on the part of public educators in Pennsylvania and Indiana because they have worried that homeschoolers could be paid for at their district's expense—and never spend a day in school.

CHANGES EXIST BEYOND STATE LEVEL

But there are other shifts as well, and they are equally significant. The U.S. Department of Education, a longtime supporter of charter schools, has issued its guidelines for charter school authorizers (U.S. Department of Education 2003). Charter school advocates relied on the department to be uncritical of their efforts. Suddenly there is a distinct change in both tone and requirements. These guidelines turn *authorizers*—formerly cheerleaders and benign observers of "their" charters—into *regulators*, a role they do not relish.

All of a sudden authorizers are confronted with educational jargon, a tangle of rules and regulations they never before confronted, as they wade through regulations they must meet to receive Title I funds. These authorizers hate being treated like public school administrators—but the new regulatory guidance puts them in that category.

AN ERA OF CRITICISM EMERGES

Reports and studies are beginning to be published that critically examine the success of charter schools in the states where they exist. Is accountability really as tight as originally promised? Have students' test scores surpassed those of their peers in comparable public schools? While advocates deny the mostly negative findings of these reports, organizations that range from the Brookings Institution to the National Education Association to the North Carolina Center for Public Policy Research are questioning the worth of charter schools as an experiment at public expense.

In North Carolina, for example, the North Carolina Center for Public Policy examined the state's charter school program, when it was five years old, and advocated that the state's cap of one hundred charter schools be retained for five more years until more data show a significant improvement between the performance of charter school students and students in traditional public schools. This has not occurred without yelps from charter advocates, who find this kind of scrutiny outrageous and demeaning.

Without question, some of the luster that seemed synonymous with charter schools in the 1990s seems a bit tarnished. But the educational bureaucracy may be missing the point—and certainly is close to missing an opportunity—when they consider the whole topic of charter schools. To understand the complexity of this issue, it is necessary to understand the types of charter schools, how they vary, and how they are staffed and organized.

WHAT IS A CHARTER SCHOOL?

Confusion reigns in almost any discussion of charter schools. Almost any gathering, whether educational or social, will illustrate that many people still do not understand—fully—what a charter school is, although they have been in existence since 1991. Some individuals may believe charters are private schools or some type of private–public hybrid. This belief is nurtured by charter advocates who promote the appearance that charters are private schools and thus offer something more special for students than what they can gain in the traditional public schools.

The whole process of getting into a charter school, wherein a student must apply for admission and be selected, supports the private school feeling. Selection carries with it a feeling of being "special," certainly more special than an average, let alone problematic, student feels in the traditional public schools. And parents feel special as well. They are involved heavily in the application process, in meetings with other parents, and in consultations with the principal and instructional staff. What they may not realize is that they are being screened, just as their child or children are being screened.

Admission Practices and "Counseling Out"

While it is illegal to deny anyone admission as long as there is physical space, charter schools screen parents quite carefully to ensure that they end up with the student body and parents that they want. They may do so by outlining a parent's responsibilities, making them more burdensome than they really are. Some charters require parents to sign a contract with the school that commits them to a certain number of unpaid hours per week, supporting the school as aides or in other capacities. They also may require parents to participate in a welter of fund-raising activities to supplement the school's budget.

As parents meet with other parents, they can find ways to "counsel them out," indicating facts about the school that make it less attractive to the prospective student and parents if the student is not, in fact, a good fit with the current or prospective population. This is particularly onerous in the case of special education, wherein charter schools may find it much easier to bounce special education students back to the home school district, using the argument that the district has more staff, has better facilities, and is more ably equipped to deal with special needs students than is the charter school (this is one instance in which the educational bureaucracy seems to be considered superior).

When parents learn their child has been accepted into a charter school, they learn *they* have been accepted. They find out that a choice and an application are reified. Finally, they have found a home—and their worries about their children will not be as severe and pressing in this personalized environment.

Setting Up a Charter School

While charter schools may give the illusion that they are private schools, they are public schools of choice. That is, they exist as publicly funded alternatives to existing public schools that serve children across the nation. They may not receive a full funding formula from the state, but they are funded through public monies.

Charter schools come into being through the acceptance of a proposal by a public charter-granting agency that may be any one of a number of agencies that sponsor the charter school, depending on the state. Proposals are initiated and written by any group interested in forming a charter school, although the specifics vary according to the legislation in different states. The groups that may want to form a charter school are interesting in their variety. Typically, they include educators who will lead and teach at the proposed school, parents who will support the school by enrolling their children and through their volunteer work, and other educational stakeholders who have a particular interest in the mission of the school.

Who Grants the Charter?

Depending on the state's legislation, the charter-granting agency might be the local school district, a university, the state department of education, or another alternative. Through a contract, or charter, the agency is charged with the responsibility of monitoring the mission, direction, and progress of the school, depending on the state in which the school is housed.

The charter school operates under the terms of the charter for a specified period of time. These lengths of time differ according to the legislation of a particular state. Most common are charters that run from three to five years, although in Arizona (one of the most pro-charter-school states) charters are granted for an unparalleled fifteen years. Typically, charters can be renewed at the end of their stipulated time.

Charter Schools Remain Popular with the Public

The U.S. Department of Education estimates that approximately 2,700 charter schools will be in operation during the academic year 2002–2003, serving an estimated 684,000 students (U.S. Department of Education 2003). The percentage of growth over the preceding year was a healthy 14 percent: enough to worry public school administrators. In states with charter schools in operation, the legislation that governs their number varies. (Some states have laws "on the books" but no charter schools. Wyoming was such a state until the 2002–2003 school year, when it finally opened its first charter school.)

Some states have placed an annual cap on the number of charter schools that may open each year; others have no limit. In some states, a cap is placed on the total number of charter schools that can operate at one time; this only changes if a charter school closes and thus opens up a slot. While charter schools are more common at the elementary level, they may exist at any level of schooling: elementary, middle, or high school, and some include all grade levels, K–12.

The Three Types of Charter Schools

Just as different agencies may hold the charter for the charter school, there are different types of charter schools, which fall into three broad categories: newly created schools, public schools that convert to charter schools, and private schools that convert to charter schools. All these schools opt for charter school status because it offers some critical factor (or many critical factors) that they cannot have within their existing schools. A key factor is generally the freedom from regulation that is extended to charter schools; in addition, private schools may welcome infusions of public funds to stay afloat. As the types of charter schools vary, so do their educational missions, values, and goals. Some rely on a back-to-basics curriculum that emphasizes direct inculcation of values; others have a vocational emphasis (usually seen at the high school level); still others (much fewer in number) are based on so-called progressive ideals.

Public or Private Administration: A Matter of Choice

Charter schools also may be administered by public or private entities. In a growing number of cases, private educational for-profit companies manage charter schools. In these cases, the advantage of a charter school is the expertise that a for-profit company can bring to the school: a well-trained principal and business manager and a well-developed curriculum. If the school does not seek autonomy in creating its own "habits of being," the for-profit option may be the best choice. Otherwise, the hiring, working conditions, and mandatory credentials of staff present another variable as these also vary from state to state.

In some charter schools, teachers must be state-certified and are subject to union regulations and protections. Others must be certified but are exempt from union regulations. Still others have provisional teaching certificates and have little or no background in education except a strong interest in teaching and some knowledge of the content area. These teachers are typically young and are "learning on the job."

Leaning on Parents

Parents are a heavily used resource at most charter schools that supplements and extends what teachers and instructional aides provide. Charter school advocates emphasize the benefits of high parental participation in the life of the school; critics applaud their presence but caution that parents may lack the expertise that qualifies them to participate in direct instruction. Some states or charter schools or both, in fact, mandate certain types of parental participation from parents if their child or children are accepted at the school (see chapter 3 for a full discussion).

While parents seem willing to provide these hours, the reason can be found in the closeness of the match between the charter school's mission and the parents' values—much like finding the "right" religious institution. Despite all the variation, however, a common characteristic of charter schools is their congruence with the values and beliefs of the families who have chosen to send their children to be educated at the school. In short, the charter schools movement can be seen as "everyone's choice"—no one in a charter school is present on an involuntary basis.

Innovation: Another Piece of Charter Rhetoric

Another appealing facet of charter schools is their apparent freedom to innovate or to implement an educational program that meets a parent's values and beliefs about education. In addition, charter schools are supposed to be held to heightened accountability and scrutiny as a condition of receiving their charters. If the goals of the charter school are not met within the time specified in the school's charter, the school can be closed (these goals typically include heightened student achievement). This part of the charter schools rhetoric is especially compelling to those who have wearied of other reform approaches to public education.

But as we shall see in chapter 3, this ability to innovate may not, in fact, be the case in most charter schools. Certain charter schools have succeeded in gaining national "star" status. Popular-media articles and other types of publicity have accompanied their innovative approach to learning, supported by heightened student achievement. Clearly, these schools are doing something right. But many other, if not most other, charter schools do not meet this goal. There is nothing particularly innovative about a charter school that seeks a back-to-basics curriculum because that is what the parent grew up with.

EVALUATING CHARTER SCHOOLS

All this diversity means that charter schools are difficult to evaluate in a comparative sense. Almost every variable that can influence student achievement can differ in charter schools, not only between charter schools and conventional public schools, but also among charter schools themselves—even in the same state. For example, students may be required to participate in the state's testing program or be recused from that requirement. If they do participate in the state's testing program, their scores may or may not be publicized, as are the scores of the students in other public schools in the states. And, as another example, the fact that for-profit, private management companies can run publicly funded charter schools—realizing a profit although the schools are publicly subsidized—is an additional complicating factor to a uniform understanding and evaluation of student achievement.

The "Choice" Argument

Advocates of choice believe that families must be able to select the school their children will attend. In its more politically controversial (and extreme) form, school choice can be represented by vouchers, which enable families to have their child educated at the public or private school of their choice at public cost. Choice advocates (who may or may not be pro-voucher) argue that if families can choose their children's schools, they can control the educational mission of the school as well as the governance and policies of the school. As a result, advocates believe that student achievement can only soar because parents and schools hold congruent goals and values.

Typically, choice advocates believe that government control of education is accompanied by cumbersome regulations that divert schools from the goals parents deem appropriate for their children. They want schools that are smaller and more responsive to their own values and goals. To those who might ask why they do not send their children to private schools that could accommodate these beliefs, these stakeholders will respond that this type of responsive schooling is a fundamental right of citizens in the United States—and that through the exercise of choice, broader reform will occur throughout the system.

Whether these advocates of choice believe in the complete privatization of education, school choice stems from arguments that public education should be privatized. The privatization of education is a concept that has had considerable appeal for nearly fifty years. In a classic article written in 1955, the Nobel Prize–winning economist Milton Friedman argued for choice options for parents and a lessened role for government in education. Friedman insisted that public schools were a fundamental right of parents and that education should be publicly funded but ultimately privatized. Although complex arguments in favor of privatization abound in the literature, a few key points are particularly relevant to charter schools, including:

- *Parents must have the right to choose their children's schools at public expense.* This view holds that the school choice option pressures low-performing schools to improve or close; it encourages wide-scale school improvement.
- *Public schools should be deregulated.* The core of the argument is that deregulation is a necessary condition of reform; freedom from bureaucratic rules and regulations must occur if schools are to be free to innovate and boost student achievement through those innovations and improvement.
- *Consumers should have direct control over the schooling their children receive.* Proponents of privatization and choice maintain that control over the nation's schools must reside with the consumer, namely, the student's parents or family members or both, and be directly responsive to their goals and values. Students are economic units. Privatization advocates believe that students will eventually become workers and must be considered public investments toward a productive future from which all citizens will benefit.
- *Education should be publicly funded but not necessarily publicly provided.* Finally, privatization advocates contend that a publicly funded service, such as education, need not be provided by the public sector (Friedman 1955).

PUBLICLY FUNDED BUT PRIVATIZED SCHOOLS

Proponents of privatization believe that a free market economy, when applied to education, will force low-performing schools to improve or lose students (customers). Proponents of choice believe that as families abandon failing schools and opt for successful schools, an increasing number of successful schools will be constructed that mesh with parental values and expectations of schooling. When this happens, failing schools will be forced to close (or in market terms, go out of business).

It is a compelling argument. But at its heart, it speaks of control, control of schooling. If a school is publicly funded, one might wonder why it would be privately managed. Pro-privatization forces would answer that the consumer, or family/student, should control the education "market" and choose whatever school is desired for the education of the student.

JUSTIFYING PUBLIC EXPENSE OF A PRIVATE EDUCATION

As Friedman (1955) articulated, pro-privatization forces also adhere to the theory that a considerable portion of the student's education—if not the entire education—should be publicly financed because an educated student eventually contributes to the economy and thus to the well-being of the nation. Because the student (product) contributes to the common good, she or he should be educated at public expense—but this should be done wherever the student's family deems best, in accordance with privately held values.

Critics of school choice believe that unless careful guidelines are applied to admissions processes, schools of choice can be inequitable. Rather than representing the larger society in which students will later function as citizens and contribute to the economy, charter schools could choose to be unresponsive to what historically has been considered a critical goal of public schooling: educating students for eventual participation in a democratic society.

And there is an interesting twist on that concern. While critics initially were concerned that charter schools could be designed for the most affluent students, usually white and middle class, and as a result, charter schools would revolve around the values of upper-middle-class, white families, another worry has emerged.

CHARTER SCHOOLS: A NEW TYPE OF "GHETTO"?

As inner-city parents of different races and ethnicities are choosing charter schools as a desperate means to extricate their children from decayed, poorly performing urban schools of poverty, some critics point to the possibility that charter schools actually may overrepresent children of color and different ethnicities. Should this happen, critics contend that a new type of educational ghetto could be formed that would be as harmful as low-performing, inner-city urban schools. At either end of the spectrum, the concern is the stratification and segregation of students in charter schools that do not reflect a representative sample of the population, along with little regard for the broader goals of democratic education.

Critics also question whether economic principles used in the private sector can be applied successfully to the public sector and, particularly, to public schools. Principles such as competition, profits, and deregulation do not strike a responsive chord with critics who believe that public schools exist for a larger, common good. They see a visceral incompatibility between the goals of public education and the means to improve it adhered to by advocates of school choice.

IS SCHOOL CHOICE DEMOCRATIC?

Another question is raised through any consideration of school choice and democracy. A fundamental difference of opinion can be seen in the concept of democracy as applied to school choice. Advocates of school choice believe that choice is profoundly democratic; critics believe it is undemocratic because it could consign students to particular schools in which they may be marginalized not only from other races and ethnicities but isolated from the goals of democratic citizenry.

DEREGULATION

Another key element of the privatization of schooling is the emphasis placed on deregulation. Advocates of privatization believe that schools should be deregulated as much as possible so that bureaucratic rules and regulations will not stultify innovation and excellence. They see government regulation of public schools as the enemy of high student achievement and teacher satisfaction.

Organizations such as teacher unions, for example, are anathema to privatization advocates because they place regulations and controls on the hiring and dismissal processes and remove that authority from the school site and from parents. In addition, the state regulates the teacher credentialing process, deciding who is qualified to teach in an effort to maintain quality control. Districts, in accordance with state finance laws, have a systematic salary schedule for teachers that typically advances via steps, a progression that corresponds to the teacher's years of experience and postgraduate education. Advocates of privatization would prefer to see all these decisions in the hands of the school site and parents.

WHO SPENDS THE MONEY?

Where there is a finite amount of money to be spent on public education, these advocates believe the decisions about how, where, and why it is spent should be made by staff at the school site in tandem with parents and families. However, they believe public funds should be used in deregulated educational settings for reasons articulated earlier in this chapter.

Although schools are governed by local school boards, adhere to district policies, and are responsive to state departments of education, privatization advocates believe that this governance should devolve directly to educational "consumers," providing consumer control of public education. Seeing parents and students as "customers," these advocates believe that most, if not all, education-related decisions should be made at the school-site level with the considerable input of parents. They decry unions, school district governance, and state department of education controls, seeing them as part of a monolithic, slow-moving machine that has contributed nothing positive to education in the past fifty years.

To buttress their arguments that consumers should control their schools in a more direct fashion, privatization advocates point to disappointing international comparisons of American student performance (Third International Mathematics and Science Study [TIMSS] 1995) and dismal achievement in poor, degrading, urban inner-city schools.

Charter schools, in part, are a reaction to vouchers. Since vouchers have become politically volatile yet have captured the commitment of a relatively narrow certain segment of the public, charter schools are a compromise between the advocates of privatization and other educational reformers who see privatization as a disastrous course.

JUSTIFYING PUBLIC FUNDS FOR PRIVATE SCHOOLS

Pro-privatization forces see no problem using public funds for deregulated schools that are responsive directly to the values and goals of parents and educators at the local site. Their logic is rather cold. They see students as cogs in the wheel, "economic units" that, if well educated, eventually will contribute to the nation's economy and thus to the common good. Friedman (1955), in his classic argument, referred to positive "neighborhood effects" that occur when properly educated youth enter the nation's workforce and contribute to the economy.

As Friedman argued, all citizens will benefit from a well-educated workforce and the United States will do well in a global economy as a result. Advocates of complete privatization agree with Friedman's contention that public dollars should be used to finance schools of choice that may be subject to other types of private input and control. This private input could include for-profit management of public schools, such as Edison, Inc., which is an alternative growing in popularity for charter schools but also growing in controversy (Doyle et al. 1994).

Privatization advocates are inclined to believe that for-profit management companies will perform better at the tasks of school management and make decisions that are fiscally sound. But if for-profit management companies do not manage schools of choice, privatization advocates maintain that parents will ensure that building-level administrators will not stray off course. It should be noted that some advocates of privatization are so completely committed to public funds used for a nongovernmental public service that they agree that even schools with a religious mission should be funded by public dollars without any attempt to regulate them.

The core argument for privatization is that education is a monopoly except for a small number of schools in the private sector, for which parents must pay. In order to exert competitive forces on the education monopoly, advocates of privatization and choice argue that the market must expand and be paid for by the government so that an adequate market exists. If there is not enough choice, a monopoly continues even if the government pays for education without providing the service (Lieberman 1989). Advocates of choice and privatization argue that the bureaucracy of government-run schooling is enormous and does not respond to the needs and values of educational consumers (parents, families, and students).

But also at the core of the argument for choice and privatization is the belief that competition between schools will result in improved student achievement (Finn, Manno, and Vanourek 2000; Lieberman 1989). This belief appears to be based on comparisons with the private sector, where if a client is dissatisfied with the services provided by an attorney or an accountant, the client will go elsewhere. But the freedom to choose services in the private sector may not reflect that alternative services are better in quality; choosing alternative services and enjoying a high degree of satisfaction with them may reflect a simple mirroring of the consumer's values—Nordstrom over Neiman Marcus.

THE RHETORIC OF THE CHARTER SCHOOLS MOVEMENT

As the preceding section demonstrates, the charter schools movement carries the weight of high hopes and the burden of charged emotions. This can be seen in the rhetoric that swirls around the charter schools movement—rhetoric that is charged with high-octane optimism. Much of it reads like promotional advertising copy, although it is issued by organizations that one might consider neutral. The tone of this rhetoric is crucial because it influences how the public regards charter schools, and it also could tilt the direction of policy.

The charter schools movement, as recently as two years ago, was characterized by a language of all or nothing: a language of polarities, a discourse of extremes. Some advocates write and speak of charter schools versus other public schools almost in terms of a zero-sum game (Center for Education Reform [CER] 2003; Finn, Manno, and Vanourek 2000; Nathan 1999). Criticisms were voiced carefully; it seemed that few wanted to go on the record as opponents of charter schools. There was a pervasive sensibility that even carefully worded caveats might offend supporters of charter schools.

Suddenly there is a shift. Critics are beginning to emerge. Whereas quite recently the rhetoric of the charter schools movement was characterized by advocacy, studies are emerging that are not unequivocally enthusiastic about charter schools. The Policy Analysis for California Education (PACE) study that pointed to less qualified teachers in charter schools, SRI's (Stanford Research Institute) decade-long study of charter schools, and recent concerns that charter schools are ending up compromising too much and accomplishing too little have muted the rhetoric. But the overwhelming tone remains positive. Perhaps because of writings of this nature, the general public is bewildered. They may not know what these schools really mean, but they think they are good, and they think they are better than noncharter public schools.

The rhetoric that surrounds charter schools points to another problem: the availability of reliable information on charter schools that parents can use to decide whether they want to enroll their children in one or whether they prefer the local public school. Information available to parents may have to be sought out; consequently, only parents who are motivated to seek an educational alternative for their child (or someone in the school system who is interested in an alternative for that child) will discover existing charter schools in the area and their admissions criteria.

While sketches of various charter schools in operation in different states are available on the Internet, those sketches typically are brief descriptions of the school's program and leave the parent alone to make a personal contact. Details of the admissions process are also not readily available. And if parents do not use computers or do not have access to computers, they could be filtered out of the information-gathering process.

The ways in which charter schools are marketed also vary by district, locality, and state. Leaders and participants in the charter schools movement show some commonly held values. These include a belief in the necessity for school choice; the importance of deregulation; the need for considerable parental involvement and decision making; the development of strong accountability for student outcomes (including heightened student achievement); the development of smaller, more personalized learning environments; and parent/local control over curriculum, assessment, and the daily conduct of the school.

A RETURN TO NOSTALGIA

At a time that is almost exactly one hundred years after the intense and lively reforms of the 1890s that continued into the 1900s, it is noteworthy that these leaders and participants in the charter schools movement seek a return to a simpler time of schooling when control was definitely local, the school's agenda was articulated and set by the parents, and there was minimal interference in the school's business from outsiders (state or federal).

There were almost no rules and regulations that had to be met in order to secure funding; a host of entitlements had not yet been crafted; and teacher unions had not yet gained their solidarity and national influence. The curriculum was much easier for parents to understand; they could participate in it quite easily with their own educational backgrounds. In many ways, the rural schools of the late 1800s match the ambitions of the charter schools movement. But to match them as cleanly and simply as that is to negate the historical events and social forces that have shaped schools within the last one hundred years.

2

HISTORICAL ACCIDENT
OR INEVITABILITY?
THE EMERGENCE
OF CHARTER SCHOOLS

The logic that underpins the charter schools movement can be considered, in part, a reaction to the course of education reform over the past one hundred years. Like many reactions, it carries the heat of considerable emotion and the conviction that it is correct.

The particular reaction that unifies the disparate group of people who have coalesced around the charter schools movement is one of wholehearted rebellion against a cumbersome bureaucracy that structures, standardizes, and controls schools. Adamant about the local control of schools, many charter school advocates point to the layers of bureaucracy that exist in any school system and protest their existence as impediments to meaningful "customer relations." Certainly the difficulty of rapid change in large urban systems has been well documented (Lockwood 1997; Finn, Manno, and Vanourek 2000; Newmann and Associates 1996; Sizer 1984), as have been the minutiae that slow the process of implementing educational innovations.

But the objections of charter school advocates extend beyond their response to local bureaucracies that they believe have impeded their right to local control—local control that is swift, bears speedy results, and is guaranteed to have power. Many charter school advocates decry the degree to which educators must demonstrate compliance with federal legislation that governs the administration of entitlements targeted to low-income and minority students, as well as students entitled to special education services. These entitlements, legislated in the 1960s and 1970s, were an integral part of the drive for equity in schooling.

Charter school advocates, however, have argued that these entitlements belong to a time when national concerns about education were different; excellence is now the issue (Finn, Manno, and Vanourek 2000; Ravitch 2000). These advocates point to the amount of local resources that is poured into demonstrating compliance with these entitlements and argue that these resources could be much better expended improving the quality and content of schooling. While charter school advocates believe federal funds should support their schools, they believe that deregulation of those funds—perhaps even complete deregulation of these funds in the form of a single block grant to states—is necessary to free up charter school operators to focus on pedagogy, curriculum, and any other goals that are part of their schools' missions.

In this chapter, we outline the development of the bureaucratic structure of schooling and the drive to standardize the nation's schools that began in the late 1800s. Next, we discuss the broad evolution of federal education policy in the last thirty years and focus on its intersection with the emergence of the charter schools movement.

THE NEED FOR STRUCTURE: DEVELOPING BUREAUCRACY AND STANDARDIZATION

Almost exactly one hundred years prior to the advent of the charter schools movement, educational reformers set a determined course to deal with the dramatic changes in American society: shifting demographics, the growth of cities, and the transition from a primarily agrarian to an industrialist society. Suddenly the norms and values of the rural schoolhouse were under close scrutiny, as prominent reformers determined that village schools would not be sufficient to prepare youth for the mechanized workplaces of the future. Just as the computer and relevant technology assumed a preeminent status in the 1980s and 1990s, the factory became the symbol of all that was efficient, progressive, and standardized. In short, it became the beacon of the mid- to late-nineteenth century, much like computer technology would become the icon of the late-twentieth and early-twenty-first century.

Reformers of the late-nineteenth century sought standardization and a staunch bureaucracy to keep quality-control measures firmly in place (as in the factory); correspondingly, reformers of the late-twentieth century looked to charter schools to carry an exhausted wave of education reform into the future—rejecting the bureaucracy and standardization that they perceived as a frustration to other education reformers. As the leaders of the charter schools movement split off from other education reformers who sought to reform the entire system, they embraced earlier values and norms that had been rejected one hundred years earlier as inefficient and insufficient.

In almost precisely a circular movement, they worked to replace professionals and their control over schooling with laypersons, sought considerably more autonomy at the school site, and demanded the devolution of decision making to the lay public. This reconfiguration insisted on placing much control of the particular charter school in the hands of parents and school-site staff; this was considered a particularly helpful innovation that would help break what charter school leaders perceived as a stranglehold by the bureaucracy.

Since the charter schools movement has been hailed as a phenomenon, singular in the history of American public education, and revelatory of its future, a few questions are worth particular scrutiny. What link can be shown between the development of the American bureaucracy of schooling and the current charter schools movement? In what ways does the evolution of the American bureaucracy of public schools explain the charter schools movement? Finally, what values relevant to public education have remained constant among the American citizenry, and what values—as demonstrated by the beliefs of those active in the charter schools movement—have shifted with the passage of time?

NOSTALGIA AND SCHOOLING

Many Americans find that they yearn for a past era of schooling when public education seemed pristine. A common perception is that at some time in American history, schooling was somehow "pure"; dominated by commonly held, decent values; and devoted to the twin goals of individual success and participation toward the common good of a democratic society. This era, in the mind of the nostalgic public, also emphasized safety, order, discipline, self-containment, and the exercise of appropriate individual ambition (Tyack 1974). In short, many members of the public perceive a time when schools performed admirably at their task of socializing students into the norms of the society of the time.

Perhaps most key, many citizens believe there was a time when public education was much less complicated—but also more successful in its admittedly more limited goals—than in the current era. These citizens view current public education as riven with dissenting reform agendas. More important, they view these reform agendas as largely unsuccessful. School staff who have experienced many waves of enthusiasm about new programs, new curriculum materials, or flavor-of-the-month reforms are wary. They are aware of the amount of energy that any innovation requires and pessimistic about a sweeping positive outcome. Finally, many members of the general public see the current public schools as impotent: splintered by a persistent lack of progress, dismal student achievement scores (particularly when viewed in international comparisons of mathematics and science), and unending, adversarial struggles over control of public education.

Like most nostalgia, this hearkening to a romantic past has been amplified by the passage of time. The history of American education is as turbulent, politicized, and marked by contradictory reform agendas as is the present. In actuality, the closest semblance to an era that many now wish to recreate dates back to the mid-1800s, when the United States was essentially an agrarian society and the common school was in a primitive form. Many have romanticized this era, although in reality it was harsh. They forget that American society in the mid to late 1800s was less complex but had a host of other difficulties. The nation's infrastructure was minimal. Rural living conditions placed a premium on hardiness, survival, and endurance. Primitive roads, crude modes of transportation, and reliance on the land (and the vagaries of weather and climate) to survive—all these factors contributed to strong communities. However, those communities existed through mutual necessity and were an automatic part of rural life. The negative aspect of this type of community was its provincialism and isolation from other people, from the immediacy of events, and from the external input of ideas and information.

Against this backdrop, Horace Mann, one of the great proponents of the common school, held lofty goals for public schools as a social institution that carried a new potential for democracy. Mann saw common schools as the enlightened vehicle that would eradicate social-class differences, educating youth at all socioeconomic levels to a common class consciousness. He believed that the mix of students of different income levels in the schools would result in an ethos of a common social class, as well as shared moral and political values (Tyack 1974). Mann, who voted for the nation's first State Board of Education, became Massachusetts's first secretary of education and worked to establish a state system of free public schools, known as common schools, which previously had been charity schools for the poor.

THE STANDARDIZATION OF THE COMMON SCHOOL

Common schools, as they evolved in the mid-1800s to late 1800s, were responsive directly to laypersons in primarily rural areas that were composed of villages and farms. Until the rise of the industrial age in the mid-1800s, which swelled to full operation by the late 1800s, American society and culture were not complex; they were dominated by an agrarian economy and primarily rural concerns. Public schooling was not compulsory; attendance was spotty; the physical condition of schoolhouses ranged from appalling to barely acceptable; and curriculum and instruction were often quixotic, at the whim of the local coterie of parents, who did not hesitate to dismiss a schoolteacher (rarely educated beyond eighth grade and occasionally less educated) who did not further their own goals and values.

Rural schools were closely allied to their particular communities. As one of few social institutions beside church, they reflected the values of the population that lived in geographic proximity. As Tyack (1974) points out, if families enjoyed congenial relationships, those relationships were reflected in school life. If, however, they quarreled, their dissension also was reflected in their difficulty reaching consensus about matters relevant to the school and the education of their children.

While Mann's goals for public schooling were ambitious and progressive, the climate of the time would not allow measures for quality control. When Mann became secretary of education in Massachusetts, his possible power was feared by rural locals who believed he would exert too much control over their schools. There also was little public agreement on the goals of public education beyond notions that schools had the potential to become a powerful social institution. While public schooling was beginning to be viewed as an unalienable "right," this right applied only to white citizens and did not typically extend to the secondary level. Even graduation from the eighth grade was considered an accomplishment (Tyack 1974).

The fragmented quality of the education delivered by mid- to late-nineteenth-century common schools is well documented (Cremin 1964; Ravitch 2000; Tyack 1974). If youths were needed to work on the family farm, they did not attend school. Or they attended school at times and not at others. There were no rules or regulations to govern their attendance or their performance. Compulsory attendance laws began to be passed in the 1850s but rarely were enforced. Similarly, there were no rules or regulations to govern the qualifications of teachers or to ensure the quality and content of the curriculum. Students were held to no external performance standards except the subjective, and the one-room schoolhouse was the most common school structure (Tyack 1974). Due to the physical conditions of the one-room schoolhouse, the schoolteacher had the challenge of simultaneously teaching a changing number of students at varying age, ability, and achievement levels (depending on enrollment and attendance), while attending to the vicissitudes of weather, physical safety in a rural environment, and similar challenges.

Gradually, due to the efforts of a coterie of education reformers, schooling began to be seen as the social mechanism that could lift young Americans to improved individual and collective futures. As the United States shifted from a predominantly agrarian to industrial society, there was a collective realization, urged and promoted by reformers, that public education in its provincial form would be inadequate for the task of preparing students for a mechanized workforce that prized efficiency and mass production. Reformers emphasized the negative: students would not be prepared for the efficiency and pace of the factory; nor would they thrive in an increasingly urban society. And reformers also emphasized the positive: schools could ameliorate the chaos of the common school and prepare students for future productive (and profitable) work lives.

Looking for solutions, reformers turned to the technology of the time to buttress their arguments. They wanted to professionalize education, to apply the rules and regulations of the factory to public schools so that education could become standardized and uniform in quality. The precision of the railroad, the efficiency and clockwork of the assembly line—these were to be emulated in the schools of the future. These reformers, who marked the 1890s with their efforts, looked at rapidly changing demographics and wanted to transform the village school to the urban school—to schools that reflected the dramatic changes in society.

Rather than continuing a version of schooling that emphasized community and local input, reformers sought an impersonal organization of schooling that would be managed by experts. Schools that were responsive solely to the needs of their village citizens were considered backward; reformers such as Elwood Cubberley bemoaned the status of public schools and urged broadscale reform. Rural schools began to be viewed as a national problem. Cubberley writes that "the schools, managed as they have been mainly by country people, are largely responsible for the condition in which country communities find themselves today, there can be little question" (Cubberley in Tyack 1974, 23).

As villages grew into cities and the populations of cities expanded rapidly, reformers were increasingly frustrated by the autonomy of local rural schools. Rural teachers continued to enjoy considerable independence from authority, parents determined the curriculum—which was directly responsive to their needs and values—and it was difficult to form a coherent, standardized policy that would extend beyond one local school to apply to other schools (Tyack 1974).

These reformers sought the "one best system" (Tyack 1974) that would work for all students. Centralized authority and layers of management dominated by experts were well-intentioned solutions to what reformers perceived as rural chaos that could not be allowed to become the structure of new urban schools. Credentials, rules, and regulations were the wave of the future. These rules and regulations, reformers maintained, would create a standardized education and layers of bureaucracy that would protect all students from the vagaries of local educational trends or whims. As Tyack writes dryly, "No detail was unimportant" (23) in the sweep toward professionalism and efficiency.

Tyack and other historians have pointed out that these reformers sought authority, buffering themselves as experts with layers of a bureaucracy that did not previously exist. They preferred that this authority be unquestioned. As a result, they worked to decrease the number of school boards in larger cities so that citizen and parent input would be less significant. Reformers believed they held the answers to the puzzle of educational reform; their solutions needed to be implemented and respected so that the country could move forward into a new economy. Rather than resting control of local schools with local communities, they contended that this control should reside with professionals who could make unbiased, expert decisions about all aspects of education. A cool sort of authoritarianism and professionalism began to prevail, dominated by credentials. Members of the general public could turn their jurisdiction over to these professionals, the reformers argued, and students could only benefit as a result.

At approximately the same time as the reform efforts of the 1890s, there was a rise of educational organizations as yet one more layer in an increasingly complex bureaucracy. These organizations were intended to further professionalize teaching and school administration. The first and perhaps most influential was the National Education Association (NEA), formed primarily for school administrators, which focused almost immediately on the "rural school problem" through its creation of an influential Committee of Twelve on Rural Schools in the 1890s. As Tyack writes:

> [T]he articulate professionals mostly agreed on the remedies: consolidation of schools and transportation of pupils, expert supervision by county superintendents, "taking the schools out of politics," professionally trained teachers, and connecting the curriculum "with the everyday life of the community." In the form of a one best system designed by professionals, the rural school would teach country children sound values and vocational skills; the result was to be a standardized, modernized "community" in which leadership came from the professionals. (1974, 23)

To gain credence as professionals, the reformers needed the unassailable foundation provided by a series of expert commissions, reports, and organizations. These commissions have exerted a pervasive influence on the course of education reform; they have packed the weight of expert opinion into their reports and exhortations.

At times, these commissions and organizations stratified teachers and administrators and brought increased adversarial relations between the groups, but they also brought them together in layers (teachers versus administrators) to solidify their activities, bringing credibility to the developing professionalism of these groups. For example, the NEA was formed originally as a professional organization for school administrators that later opened its ranks to teachers—but they were in the union on the union's terms (Urban in Lockwood 1997). The American Federation of Teachers (AFT), on the other hand, was formed by and for high school teachers and stayed under their control through the 1940s and 1950s. An "us against them" mentality between administrators and teachers had early and forceful roots that have persisted to the current era of reform.

The rhetoric and goals of standardization were not effective with most rural citizens. In fact, the "professional reforms" that began in the 1890s were decidedly unpopular. The consolidation of rural schools—an efficiency and quality movement—became a battle, as rural residents struggled to maintain local control over their schools. These residents disliked the idea of sending their children to consolidated schools where the schools were under a centralized control such as the county superintendent of schools, and their own input would be limited. They saw little or no reason to give up the easy familiarity of community—however provincial it might seem to outsiders—in favor of impersonal and businesslike schooling practices.

Of course, the nation had been shifting to an industrialized society since the mid-1800s. As cities and villages expanded, schools were becoming more complex and in need of organization. From 1870 to 1898, the number of students enrolled in public schools increased from less than 7 million to approximately 15 million, although the information about schools (and therefore statistics on students) was unreliable. Expenditures also rose from $63 million per year to $199 million per year during the same time period. Meanwhile, the typical length of time a student spent in school was only five years (Tyack 1974, 66).

To reformers, these statistics were heady proof that their efforts were on course. Since compulsory schooling laws were not enforced on any regular basis, they saw the commitment to approximately five years of education as a sign that the public agreed that schooling was important. Fueled by the rapid population expansion and migration to cities, they asserted the need for a strong central organization of schools and structures where roles would be clear and static, once established. Additional proof of public support of schools came from funding: during the latter half of the nineteenth century, more than two-thirds of public funds for schools came from local tax assessments (Tyack 1974).

The reformers of this era were absolutists in their beliefs. In preparing students for the mechanized workplaces of the future, submission and conformity became standard expectations. Attendance, punctuality, and respect for authority, as well as many other characteristics valued in the factory mode of production, became a part of the "hidden curriculum." As William T. Harris, St. Louis superintendent of schools and later U.S. commissioner of education, articulated: "The first requisite of the school is *Order*, each pupil must be taught first and foremost to conform his behavior to a general standard" (Tyack 1974, 43). Harris, a widely respected intellectual, took on the charge to reform public education and became a leading progressive figure in the twentieth century.

In a relatively brief period of time, urban school leaders rose to the challenge, creating systems that mimicked contemporary industry. Cities were divided into districts; schools into grade levels; teachers were required to seek training relevant to their task and also certification to do their work; the curriculum became a sequence; and tests (woefully inadequate) began to be devised to ascertain student progress. A set of textbooks was prescribed and followed. All sorts of unchallenged reasons for the ways in which schools conducted their business became the norm (Oakes 1985; Tyack 1974).

Just as the NEA's Committee of Twelve on Rural Schools dictated certain courses of action to standardize rural schools with the goal of wide-scale improvement, the NEA's powerful Committee of Ten on Secondary Studies was formed to recommend actions that would standardize secondary schools' college-preparatory curricula and colleges' admissions requirements (Oakes 1985, 17). The Committee of Ten, under the leadership of Harvard University president Charles Eliot, recommended a restructuring of the secondary school curriculum into four strands, each of which would be acceptable for college admission: classical, Latin-scientific, modern languages, and English (Oakes 1985). Each of the four strands was deemed equally worthy, and the committee concurred that students should not be separated into college-preparatory and vocational tracks.

At approximately the same time—the beginning of the 1900s—the tide of immigration began to rise. Intermediate schools had already been formed for poor and immigrant children who did not meet entrance requirements of grade schools; these schools increased in number as the numbers of immigrants began to swell and public alarm about their entry into the United States increased. These special schools negated previous informal policy through which the curriculum of the common elementary school had been universal for all students, a basic array of reading, writing, spelling, arithmetic, geography, and Bible reading (Oakes 1985).

Widespread anxiety about changing demographics, particularly about immigrants from southern and eastern Europe, began to spread. At a rate of nearly 1 million people per year, immigrants continued to arrive in the United States from southern and eastern Europe (Oakes 1985). By 1924, approximately 24 million of these immigrants had settled into American life (Oakes 1985). They were in flight from intolerable living conditions in other countries but were unskilled and, for the most part, uneducated. As a result, they settled for unskilled work in urban areas where living conditions were overcrowded and dirty—the only living conditions they could afford. Jobs were not plentiful; immigrants were competing with the increasing number of rural citizens who had left agrarian life for an improved future in the city.

Because of their socioeconomic status, their living conditions, and their "foreignness," these immigrants and their children endured considerable discrimination. School leaders believed it was the duty of the public schools to reduce group and individual differences and blend immigrants into a homogeneous American society. Immigrants assumed a hopeful posture: schools would enable them to assimilate into American society and find their way to improved economic futures. They viewed school "professionals" respectfully and did not challenge their edicts and decisions but deferred to their judgment. Because of their entry-level status in American culture, immigrants bent to what one of the nation's most powerful social institutions thought was good for them: assimilation.

In turn, the public schools served as a type of settlement house, melding outsider youths into a seamless group with distinct, accepted roles. Meanwhile, nonimmigrant youths continued to be served by the schools in ways that separated them from immigrants. Reformers pounced on the curriculum in secondary schools and began to call for as much differentiation as possible. This differentiation was intended to serve young people as appropriately and precisely as possible and to prepare them for eventual roles in the workforce or, for the few, admission to college. However, extensive differentiation of the curriculum and the resulting stratification of students into distinct tracks led to an increasingly disjointed and fragmented quality of school life. The differentiated curriculum, with its many tracks and slots, also was a convenient school structure that helped when school staff searched for a place for immigrant children who were not an immediate fit with the school, due to language or other issues.

Schools dominated by several tracks split any sense of community that smaller and less curricularly fragmented schools used to possess—both for students and for staff and, particularly, at the secondary level. While reformers urged curricula that were tailor-made for different students, they also encouraged the development of rigid school structures that later would be decried by more than one generation of education reformers and proved difficult to undo (Oakes 1985).

Along with the assignment into tracks that featured different emphases, such as college preparatory course work or vocational preparation (usually manual training of some kind), came expectations for eventual positions in society. Gone was Horace Mann's notion of the common school as an equalizing force between different social classes. In place was a type of sorting machine: a streamlined factory producing students equipped for very distinct roles in society. The future factory manager, the assembly line worker, the professor—all had a track in the American secondary school that differentiated, sorted, and assigned their eventual place in society.

One of the most troublesome parts of these tracks was their lack of fluidity. Once assigned to a vocational track, for example, a student had little chance of leaving it for a college preparatory track. Assignments could be arbitrary, based on test scores or teacher perceptions. And these assignments preceded eventual workplace slots that also were static and unyielding.

Reformers were pleased at the progress of the secondary school in the early 1900s. It offered something for everyone (Oakes 1985). By the time large comprehensive high schools were firmly entrenched in American society, the selection of course offerings and tracks was almost dazzling in its variety—except that choice of track was not student or family determined, but school driven.

Matching the emphasis on scientific knowledge and professionalism, various social theories flourished, all of which had a profound influence on the course of education reform in the twentieth century. The theories of Charles Darwin gave scientific credence to the notion that some groups were destined to be inferior to others. While immigrants who lived in squalid conditions had no economic choice, they were seen as responsible for their plight, even depraved (Oakes 1985). Psychologists began to formulate concepts of intelligence and intelligence-testing assessments (IQ tests) to sort more precisely and assess the ability of students.

At the same time that the scientific, professional reformers were making major structural and curricular changes in the nation's schools, John Dewey was rising to prominence as a well-respected reformer, a spokesperson for so-called progressivism. In his work, Dewey called for a connection between education and democracy, especially in light of the new social order brought about by the effects of immigration. He wrote that

a government resting upon popular suffrage cannot be successful unless those who elect and who obey their governors are educated. Since a democratic society repudiates the principle of external authority, it must find a substitute in voluntary disposition and interest; these can be created only by education. But there is a deeper explanation. A democracy is more than a form of government; it is primarily a mode of associated living, of conjoint communicated experience. The extension in space of the number of individuals who participate in an interest so that each has to refer his own action to that of others . . . is equivalent to the breaking down of those barriers of class, race, and national territory which kept men from perceiving the full import of their activity. (Dewey in Cremin 1964, 121–122)

Instead of viewing education as prevocational training or a narrow set of experiences that prepares youth for their choice of occupation,

Dewey urged a larger conception of education, one in which the individual makes enlightened social choices and is educated to make such choices (Cremin 1964, 123). While he found vocational preparation useful, he only applauded it when it was subordinate to what he called "intellectual results and the forming of a socialized disposition" (Dewey in Cremin 1964, 124–125). He decried class differences as evidenced in educational preparation, such as the practice of reserving the study of classics for wealthier groups of students. He also believed that all students should experience a mixture of vocational and intellectual work to prepare them for participation in a democratic society. As he wrote, "A democracy cannot flourish where there is narrowly utilitarian education for one class and broadly liberal education for another" (Dewey in Cremin 1964, 125).

Dewey also realized that the school was poised to replace the family as the primary shaping mechanism that would socialize and prepare youth (Ravitch 2000, 369). He viewed this as progressive; the school would ameliorate negative family influences and shape the student for full participation in a democratic society. It would lie within the grasp of each student to hold high personal goals. It then would be the school's responsibility—even its "sacred" right—to facilitate the accomplishment of those goals.

Dewey had a significant impact on the education that would follow in the twentieth century, particularly in the 1960s and 1970s, when dispossessed groups began to assert their rights. A band of reformers adopted his beliefs in the 1930s, pushing goals for democratic education and arguing against narrow stratification of the curriculum. Nonetheless, an ongoing tension between proponents of curriculum differentiation and so-called progressivism continued with no resolution to the debate. By now, the bureaucracy was well formed and securely established.

As the twentieth century progressed, a link between the degree of education a student attained and the student's eventual success in society began to be drawn. Success in school correlated with college entrance and prestigious places in the workforce. One study conducted in 1940 asked employers in eighteen industries the minimum educational level they required of potential hires (Tyack 1974, 273). The study found that the degree of schooling correlated with white-collar occupations. Persons hired as managers, clerks, and sales workers needed a high school graduation while a majority of workers hired as professionals or semi-professionals required a college degree (Tyack 1974, 273).

Yet schooling had not accomplished its democratic aim of educating all children. Enormous inequities existed in financing and in segregated school systems in the South. In 1940, 20 million children aged six to fifteen were not enrolled in any school (Tyack 1974, 273). Differences in financing showed a lack of progress toward equity—not to mention sufficiency of funding. In 1939–1940 approximately 19,500 children attended schools that cost $6,000 per classroom; twice that number attended schools where the unit cost was less than $100. The top percentage of the nation's schools spent approximately $4,115 while the lowest percentage spent $500 (Tyack 1974, 273). These severe discrepancies were permitted by law. Schools for black students had a median expense of $477 (Tyack 1974, 273).

In the late 1940s, educational strategy began to be dominated by concern about the Cold War and a resurgence in democratic goals for the education of all children—but couched in the adversarial rhetoric of the Cold War. While the Great Depression and World War II had broken the progress of education reform, now the public began to unite through fear that was fueled by national leaders. They shared in an abiding concern that the United States would lag behind Communist countries (particularly the Soviet Union) and in a determination (expressed by national leaders) that America's children must be prepared to compete intellectually and economically with the Soviets. Technological dominance became an issue of considerable debate in educational circles, as did the best path to improving mathematics and science achievement.

Meanwhile, many special interest groups joined the battle for adequate and equitable financing for the nation's schools as well as for credentialed teachers (because of World War II, the 1940s had seen an unprecedented teacher shortage). Groups such as the National Association of Manufacturers and the Chamber of Commerce joined what had been purely an educational issue and lent weight to the argument that future workers would enjoy higher incomes if they had more education (Tyack 1974, 275). Their participation, as well as that of organizations such as the American Federation of Labor and the Congress of Industrial Organizations (AFL-CIO), enlarged the economic argument for more education for more students. As much education as possible, for as many students as possible, began to be seen as essential to the full development of a democratic society that could engage in competition in the international arena and enjoin in the Cold War.

But the sweeping events of the mid-1900s had passed over the poor and members of minority groups. As Tyack points out, "During one year of World War II *the United States spent more for military purposes than it had expended on public education during the entire history of the nation*" (1974, 275, italics mine). And during the 1950s, although the nation apparently coalesced in a triumphant surge of Cold War sentiment, many in educational circles fell by the wayside due to McCarthyism—a victory of local control married to national rhetoric. Politically outspoken teachers were fired without recourse; students were taught a type of "groupthink" about the nation and its Communist opponents that encouraged passivity.

Yet by 1960 the public schools had accomplished nothing less than a revolution in less than one hundred years, as evidenced by a few statistics:

- In 1960, over 46 million students were in school, composed of approximately 99.5 percent of children aged seven to thirteen, 90.3 percent of those aged fourteen to seventeen, and 38.4 percent of those aged eighteen and nineteen.
- In 1966, 93.4 percent of all public school teachers had bachelor's degrees or additional postsecondary education.
- Pupil–teacher ratios were far less than in 1910, and federal and state aid were expanding funds available to public schools. (Tyack 1974, 269)

THE GREAT SOCIETY: DEVELOPING FEDERAL EDUCATION POLICY

Federal education policy began to emerge as the societal upheaval of the 1960s banished the Cold War from public consciousness. The first major event to bring equity to the forefront occurred in the 1950s with the 1954 case of *Brown v. Board of Education* (347 U.S. 483). In this landmark case, the United States Supreme Court ruled that separate was not equal, which meant that racially segregated schools were unconstitutional. The federal government became involved in enforcing desegregation measures; as black students began to be assimilated into all-white schools, there was considerable societal tension and anger, particularly in the South.

In 1954, when the *Brown* decision was enacted, nearly 10 million students were enrolled in the nation's schools, including approximately 3.4 million black students. The schools included racially segregated schools that existed by law in seventeen states and Washington, D.C.—with segregated schools tolerated in an additional four states (Ravitch 2000, 372). As the segregated southern states dodged the implications of the *Brown* decision for a number of years, the disparities between the education available to white citizens and to black citizens were severe. And while southern states, eager to retain racial segregation in their schools, sought to diminish inequities by infusing monies into schools for black citizens, it was impossible to make up for a long history of neglect (Ravitch 2000).

As the nation entered the 1960s, there was increasing attention to equity, to the plight of the poor, and to members of minority groups. This was brought about at least in part by the large numbers of black people who migrated to northern states from the South between 1940 and 1960. In those twenty years, over 3 million blacks abandoned the South for the North; large numbers chose to live in cities, a growth from 49 percent in 1940 to 73 percent in 1960 (Ravitch 2000, 376). Just like the tidal wave of immigrants who came to the United States between 1900 and 1924, black people lived in substandard housing conditions. They lived in communities that for all practical purposes were racially segregated, and they attended all-black schools (that were not technically racially segregated). This infusion of blacks into northern cities saw the phenomenon of white flight, as urban whites fled to the suburbs. White flight resulted in even more inequitable school-financing formulas, as resources drained from what began to be known as "inner cities" and funds were infused in primarily white, suburban schools.

Members of black groups as well as other minority groups became increasingly vocal, unwilling to continue to be ignored and, worse, actively discriminated against in social practices such as schooling. The civil rights movement carried the frustrations and hopes of a large segment of the population who were unwilling to continue their disenfranchised status. The consequences of their active presence on the national political stage had important effects on the development of a federal education policy and the emergence of the U.S. Department of Education.

The U.S. Department of Education is relatively young as a federal department bearing cabinet status, although its roots sink deeply into the nineteenth century. President Andrew Johnson established the first Department of Education in 1867. The department was not at the cabinet level and lasted less than a year. Its main task was to collect statistics about the nation's schools. Its brief presence can be explained by the widespread fear that it would become too powerful and exert too much influence over the nation's schools. The Department of Education was changed to the Office of Education and, as such, had little real power or direct influence on the shaping of federal education policy.

The Department of Education did not appear again until 1979, when Congress passed Public Law 96-98 establishing the department. The Department of Education was granted cabinet status in 1981. The major responsibilities given to the department are

- establishing policies related to financial aid for education, administering the distribution of these funds, and monitoring their use;
- collecting data and overseeing research on America's schools and disseminating this information to the public;
- identifying major issues and problems in education and focusing attention on these problems;
- enforcing federal statutes prohibiting discrimination in programs and activities receiving federal funds and ensuring equal access to education.

During the Clinton presidency, a strategy aimed at improving the nation's schools and making them more accountable for student outcomes was enacted, called America 2000. This four-part strategy was built on the foundation of the Goals 2000 that emerged from the National Education Summit of 1989, when George H. Bush was president.

His son, President George W. Bush (Bush), enacted the most sweeping reauthorization of the 1965 Elementary and Secondary Education

Act (ESEA) this country has seen, calling it "No Child Left Behind." In the No Child Left Behind (NCLB) legislation, which immediately angered public educators, considerable emphasis is placed on increasing accountability without much guidance about how to achieve heightened student achievement.

The NCLB legislation hit the educational community with a jolt. Instead of simply reauthorizing the long-standing, familiar ESEA legislation, the Bush administration caught the educational community off guard with its aggressive No Child Left Behind rewrite of this historical legislation. The fact that conservative Republicans and liberal Democrats alike embraced the legislation added to the educators' confusion. While nobody could or would question the sentiment of "no child left behind," educators had long taken it for granted that ESEA was primarily concerned with providing compensatory services to the economically disadvantaged. The sense on the part of most educators was that ESEA was an effort to level the playing field for children at risk of failing in public schools.

The legislation was never fully funded, the challenge was generally seen as greater than the schools' ability to address it, and the ever-increasing numbers of at-risk children seemed to suggest that educators were expected to address—but not turn around—the plight of poor children. Then NCLB came into being and the unwritten expectations changed overnight. Now those who accepted federal money were told they were going to be held accountable for raising student achievement for all children and in particular those traditionally left behind by the public schools. Schools must provide all children with quality teachers and ensure adequate yearly progress in student achievement or provide parents with a broad choice of schools where expectations could be met.

The NCLB legislation undoubtedly will accomplish two principal aims of the Bush administration. One, it will for the first time give the public access to data that will showcase both quality and low-quality schools. The public will know, for instance, where the less-qualified teachers work. In fact, schools will be forced to notify parents if their children are being taught in a classroom served by an unqualified teacher. Parents who wish to transfer their students from such an environment will have broad choices of alternative public schools to attend, at the district's expense.

Parents with children in what have passed for "quality schools" will now know the extent to which subsets of students are well served or not. The NCLB requires the district to keep student achievement data for racial groups as well as developmentally challenged students. If the school is unable to show adequate yearly progress in all subgroups, the school itself will be found wanting.

Educators complain that NCLB is an unrealistic law because it does not provide the schools with adequate resources to address the challenge of educating all students to high standards. That is a valid complaint, but it misses the point. The fact is educators have, for a variety of reasons, long saddled the children with the greatest needs with the district's least well-trained teachers. The backers of NCLB say it is time that children in low-performing schools get the same quality teachers as in schools serving the affluent. The educators respond by saying they hire the best teachers they can. Even when quality teachers are placed in hard-to-staff schools serving poor and minority students, they tend to quit or leave in disproportionate numbers for schools with higher-achieving students. But how do districts attract and retain quality teachers in hard-to-staff schools? Until educators figure out an answer to that question, NCLB provisions promise to seriously erode public confidence in public schools.

And to many educational pundits, that is the second major legislative goal of the Bush administration: to demonstrate publicly and loudly that the nation's public schools take over $10 billion of taxpayers' money each year for compensatory education and fail to deliver the goods. The solution? Vouchers, of course, with more charter schools, at a minimum. Educators worry that the administration will argue that public schools cannot ensure a quality educator for all students, and therefore parents should be given options. Vouchers that parents can use to enroll their students in schools of their choice would be high on the Bush administration's priority list. But short of that, politicians from both parties suggest that charter schools are a logical alternative to low-performing public schools.

EQUITY AND THE NATION'S SCHOOLS

As Diane Ravitch has pointed out, what we think of when we consider the 1960s as an era of social unrest did not really conclude until the end of the Nixon presidency in the mid-1970s (Ravitch 2000, 367). And the nation's schools became an arena in which many social conflicts ended up being played out during this long period of time. Several assassinations, the civil rights movement, the Vietnam War, and the Watergate era coalesced to constitute a time of social ferment and unrest.

In 1964, President Lyndon Johnson, empowered by the landslide that elected him to the presidency that same year, brought his considerable political power to bear on two remarkable efforts: the passage of the Civil Rights Act and the War on Poverty. As a part of the War on Poverty, Johnson pushed the 1965 ESEA through Congress. Billions of dollars were poured into entitlements and programs targeted at low-income students and students of color who were lagging far behind their peers in academic achievement. Title I, the longest running and best known of the entitlements, provided approximately $12 billion per year in funding toward educational services for children of poverty.

The belief at the time—although not devoid of controversy—was that inputs, such as money put into schools that would equalize financing formulas, would affect student achievement positively and reduce wide discrepancies caused by uneven resource allocation. The educational services that students served by Title I typically received in the 1960s, 1970s, and 1980s were compensatory in nature. From the inception of ESEA, the focus was on the delivery of remedial services to low-income students lagging behind in academic achievement, usually delivered through a series of pullout programs during the school day. These pullout programs had an unfortunate consequence of stigmatizing the students who received special services.

There is current consensus among reformers and researchers that the model of compensatory education offered by Title I has been unsuccessful (Finn, Manno, and Vanourek 2000; Slavin 1997). Considerable debate, however, exists about what strategies would improve the efficacy of Title I monies, and there is also controversy about whether Title I monies should continue to be targeted to children of poverty. Current reformers such as Robert Slavin at Johns Hopkins University advocate the use of a comprehensive reform model in Title I schools. A current federal push is to support comprehensive reform models that take into consideration the governance of the school, social services delivery, an integrated curriculum, heavy doses of professional development that connect with the comprehensive reform model, and regular assessments of student progress.

In 1966, the year after the passage of ESEA, James Coleman, a sociologist at the University of Chicago, and a team of scholars published what came to be known as "the Coleman report." This major federal study, *Equality of Educational Opportunity*, jolted the educational community. Coleman and his colleagues found that schools had relatively little influence on students' futures, goals, and aspirations—and that their families and/or peers were much more influential.

Because of his belief in peer influences, Coleman became an advocate of racial integration in the nation's schools with the proviso that disadvantaged students would be melded into schools of majority populations of white, middle-class students (Ravitch 2000, 415). Court-ordered busing became an action mandated in many school districts across the United States as educators attempted to ameliorate the odds that many students simply would not succeed in life given the student composition of their schools (inner-city, black, poor) and their family characteristics.

In 1981 Coleman changed his position in a major federal study of public and private schools. In particular, he argued that Catholic schools or other private schools did a superior job educating students of all economic and racial backgrounds because they held students to high academic expectations and taught a common academic curriculum (Ravitch 2000). Coleman and others pointed to the ethos that permeated private schools, particularly Catholic schools, that created a culture of courtesy and mutual respect. As a result, leading reformers began to talk about and research the need for "professional community" and other types of community in large, impersonal comprehensive high schools (Newmann and Associates 1996).

Most members of the public agree that the 1960s and 1970s were an era of social revolution and unrest. Nowhere was this more apparent than in the nation's schools. The Cold War emphasis on docile behavior and achievement yielded to students' rights, demonstrations, arguments for "relevant" studies, and what many view as a diminishment of teachers' authority or what Kevin Ryan calls a "moral compass" (Ryan in Lockwood 1997). As the 1960s yielded to the 1970s, urban schools saw riots and acts of violence that frightened school staff, parents, and students. Compared with the staid school climates of the 1950s and early 1960s, schools seemed to have given way to a new standard of societal disarray. Fearful of lawsuits, school administrators and teachers became wary of exerting their authority. Simultaneously, school staff nationwide endured a rapid-fire succession of reform-based programs, some with dubious merit. Lack of consistency, uneven funding streams, and failure to commit sufficient time all contributed to the demise of these programs and the growing cynicism of school staff about whether external reforms would be effective.

Alternative schools began to mushroom, founded by former social activists who decried "the system." Schools for students who were difficult to teach, for students on the verge of dropping out, and for students who wanted a purely vocational curriculum all began to burgeon as part of local school systems. These alternative schools had difficulty gaining academic legitimacy but remained a mechanism that took pressure off the larger system. If potential dropouts and discipline problems could be educated together in small schools that were designed just for them, other schools would have fewer discipline problems to disrupt the school day. These schools, however, continued to contribute to the public perception that the public school system was in disarray.

The most recent, significant shift in educational goals occurred early in the Reagan administration and was codified with the publication of *A Nation at Risk* (National Commission on Excellence in Education 1983 [National Commission 1983]). That now classic report, issued by the U.S. Department of Education under the direction of Secretary of Education Terrence Bell, warned of a "rising tide of mediocrity" that threatened to swamp the nation's schools. It pointed to sinking achievement on the part of American students, particularly when viewed in the context of international comparisons. The report's rhetoric was severe and urgent; the authors warned that the nation's "once unchallenged preeminence in commerce, industry, science, and technological innovation is being overtaken by competitors throughout the world" (National Commission 1983). Letting the achievement of American youth slip to the level of mediocrity, chided the report's authors, had been a type of "educational disarmament" (National Commission 1983).

The goals articulated in *A Nation at Risk* (National Commission 1983) dwelled on the nation's need to ready itself for the future, a brutally competitive future dominated by high technology and a fierce global economy. Existing, not to mention competing, in this new society would

be difficult, the authors cautioned, even with the best education designed specifically to equip new workers in technologically sophisticated
workplaces that would demand intricate problem-solving skills. They
cited a 1982 Gallup poll in which citizens rated education as the major
foundation for all other efforts, including "the best industrial system" or
"the strongest military force." In an ironic tone, the authors referred to
the nation's culture of "minimum requirements" and urged educational
reformers to bring rigor to public education.

The publication of A Nation at Risk (National Commission 1983) ushered in the beginnings of the "excellence" era, or a reaction to the years
in which the federal government invested heavily in programs targeted
to further educational equity, beginning with the Johnson administration. While it is beyond the scope of this book to debate the "equity
versus excellence" movement, a few points are relevant directly to the
development and appeal of charter schools. A Nation at Risk's goals are
of keen interest both historically and because they provide a dramatic
contrast to the open education offered in the late 1960s and the individually centered instruction favored in the 1970s.

The report's authors functioned almost as trend forecasters. Just
ahead of the spirit of the times, they publicized a growing sense of new
conservatism and concern that the United States would not be able to
maintain economic preeminence internationally. The report hinted at
the drive toward national standards for content and performance that
would follow in the late 1980s and 1990s. Finally, the report brought on
a national anxiety among educational researchers about educational performance of the nation's students—and ushered in feelings of inade-
quacy that became the wellspring for many education reforms.

At another level, the report reflected a growing "culture of narcissism" that focused on the acquisition of the material and the value of
wealth (Lasch 1978). Rather than articulating social goals that might
promote educating for democracy, or educating for participation in a
democratic society, A Nation at Risk (National Commission 1983) articulated goals more focused, limited, and specific.

Two especially revealing sentences from the report are harbingers of
the reform movement that followed and the drive toward educational
alternatives such as charter schools:

Citizens know intuitively what some of the best economists have shown in their research, that education is one of the chief engines of a society's well-being. They know, too, that education is the common bond of a pluralistic society and helps tie us to other cultures around the globe. (National Commission 1983)

The emphasis on education tied to participation in the workforce, the United States' competition in a global economy, and references to the material success of citizens tell the concerns of the time, along with the acknowledgment that the nation was rapidly becoming more racially, ethnically, and socioeconomically diverse. These concerns foreshadowed the preoccupation of policymakers during the 1980s and 1990s (through the Clinton administration) that the United States lagged behind internationally, a concern supported by disappointing achievement test scores in view of international comparisons (TIMSS 1995).

Contrasted to the concerns and goals of Lyndon Johnson's Great Society, which sought educational equity for all citizens, educational policy twenty years later was devolving toward the individual, the competitive, and the material. The common good was defined as success in a global economy and the career success of the individual; the nation's leaders joined with corporate executives to map out a plan not for educational equity of opportunity, but for equal opportunity to compete internationally to net better profits.

The emphasis on global competition and workforce readiness continued as a major thrust in the education reform movement. In 1989, President George H. Bush convened the National Governors Summit to discuss the future of American education. This summit, considered historic by many, resulted in what came to be called "Goals 2000" and the Goals 2000: Educate America Act legislation, which was enacted under President Bill Clinton (governor of Arkansas at the time of the National Governors Summit).

Three National Education Summits were held during the George H. Bush administration and then the Clinton administration. The first summit, the National Governors Summit, led to an agreement to adopt a challenging set of national education goals. At this summit, George H. Bush emphasized in his remarks that the standards would be national, not federal, a concern of the people in many states who feared federal control of education.

The eight goals were ambitious and included the following:

1. Ready to Learn (Every child shall enter school ready to learn).
2. School Completion.
3. Student Achievement and Citizenship.
4. Teacher Education and Professional Development.
5. Mathematics and Science.
6. Adult Literacy and Lifelong Learning.
7. Safe, Disciplined, and Alcohol- and Drug-Free Schools.
8. Parental Participation. (U.S. Department of Education 1998)

The second National Education Summit, held in 1996, resulted in a commitment by governors to enact high academic standards in their individual states (this marked a shift from the national standards movement to the state level). The third National Education Summit, held in 1999, focused on the need to find strategies to implement standards-based reform. Six organizations cosponsored the group; again there was heavy input from the corporate sector, including the Business Roundtable and the National Alliance of Business, respectively.

The focus on developing competencies specific to the workplace continued to accelerate. In 1991, the secretary of labor appointed the Secretary's Commission on Achieving Necessary Skills (SCANS) to discern what skills and competencies the nation's youth needed to be prepared fully for entry into the workforce. The commission's primary purpose was to "encourage a high-performance economy characterized by high-skill, high-wage employment" (SCANS 1991). The connection with education, the commission declared, was to help teachers understand the ways in which curricula and pedagogy should change so that students would develop "high-performance" skills needed to succeed in the "high-performance workplace."

The commission outlined basic skills, thinking skills, and personal qualities in addition to five workplace "competencies" that ranged from the use of resources to interpersonal qualities to the ability to work with a variety of technologies. Basic skills included reading, writing, arithmetic/mathematics, listening, and speaking. Thinking skills integrated creative thinking, decision making, and ability to reason. Personal qualities included responsibility, self-esteem, sociability, self-management, and integrity and honesty.

An emphasis on the practical can be seen throughout these skills. Under the "writing skill," for example, the documents the student should be able to produce include letters, directions, manuals, reports, graphs, and flowcharts. Thinking skills carry a similar emphasis: "seeing things in the mind's eye," for instance, portrays the student as one who effectively "organizes, and processes symbols, pictures, graphs, objects, and other information." Personal qualities seem dominated by sociability, or "understanding, friendliness, adaptability, and empathy."

The five workplace competencies are similarly pragmatic in bent. The "resources" category is similar to the other four competencies. The student should be able to deal with money successfully, for example, preparing budgets, making forecasts, and keeping records. Although these skills and competencies were developed with the workplace firmly in mind, they were intended to influence and change basic curriculum and instruction in the nation's schools.

The qualities and attributes of remarkable people are not included in these skills and competencies. There is no mention of leadership qualities, no mention of the ability to motivate and influence others, and scant mention of creativity. Problem solving is consigned to the rote management of workplace problems; congeniality is prized. This emphasis reflects an essentially flat workplace with workers who are placed laterally. These workers must be able to deal with technology and customers alike. The qualities of the outstanding scientist, the senator, the musician, creative artist, poet, architect, or mathematician are not reflected.

Viewed in this context, charter schools are not a historical oddity or accident. Perhaps they were an inevitability. Charter schools effectively separated themselves from the contemporary version of the common school to honor individually held values and uphold the private educational visions of parents and educators. These educational visions appear to center on preparation for the workforce or admission to competitive colleges or both so that prospective workers can gain a higher foothold in the future workplace. The additional inculcation of "values" traditionally learned in the extended family or more attention to traditional socialization into conventional societal norms also became a mainstay of the attractiveness of the charter schools movement, at least to many educational consumers.

By the time *A Nation at Risk* (National Commission) was published in 1983, a new era of contentious reform had begun: a battle over equity versus excellence. Coleman's influential findings in 1981, along with a national movement toward high standards for all students, led reformers to call for massive changes in schooling. Reformers continued to seek and want federal dollars in support of their reform proposals and their programs but began to argue for new conceptions of federal educational policy. Ideas such as vouchers, state control of federal funds, and streamlined reporting guidelines began to gain currency in the reform literature. Notions such as the need to "restructure" schools, which focused on a systemic approach that welded grassroots reform to top-down mandates, became popular.

In sharp contrast to the actions of the reformers of the late 1800s, who saw a need to professionalize public schooling through the creation of a bureaucracy that standardized education for all students, the reform movement of the 1980s and 1990s began to pull away from the idea of a bureaucracy as helpful to education reform. Instead, reformers began to dwell on the importance of high academic "standards" for content and performance, the need for "empowering" teachers, the need for high-quality, sustained professional development, and the need for educational experiments that would be supported by the public system, such as charter schools and vouchers. Big government, as reflected in federal infusions of funds into public education, began to be viewed with suspicion. Some reformers even considered federal policy or legislation as attempts to control or even subvert education. As federal goals for the nation's schools developed in the late 1980s and 1990s, it was clear that the pendulum had swung away from an emphasis on equity to an emphasis on quality and excellence.

THE NEED FOR STANDARDS AND ALTERNATIVES

In growing frustration with what they perceived as lack of progress as evidenced in the students' achievement scores on standardized tests, many reformers began to unite around the need for standards—but they coupled this with the need for deregulated publicly funded alternatives. They argued that there should be high academic expectations for all students, and that these expectations would become a self-fulfilling prophecy. They also contended that the "system" was so deeply flawed that the best choice was to become a type of educational pioneer and create a new school from the ground up. One way to do this was through the creation of a charter school.

Charter schools became an alternative that was greeted with enthusiasm in most quarters. Understandably, teacher unions hesitated (even though Al Shanker of the AFT was an early figure in the charter schools movement) because of the possible repercussions for their members who might be interested in teaching in largely deregulated charter schools. A relatively small segment of reformers and researchers whose work centered on equity expressed reservations, mostly focused on equity aspects of this new educational alternative (see, for example, Wells et al. 1998). Meanwhile, charter schools legislation continued to burgeon in a number of states. The wide array of support for these schools surprised critics. In 1998, Clinton signed into law the Charter School Expansion Act of 1998, with the expressed goal of three thousand charter schools operating early in the twenty-first century. In his statement, Clinton said that "this bill will help strengthen our efforts to support charter schools, providing parents and students with better schools, more choice, and higher levels of accountability in public education" (U.S. Department of Education 1998).

Conservative reformers indicted previous federal education policy as they continued to support the expansion and growth of charter schools as the most promising educational reform on the national landscape. One of the leading advocates of charter schools, Chester E. Finn Jr., argues that equality of opportunity—or equal access to education—"has now largely been accomplished" (Kanstoroom and Finn 1999). He contends that equity is no longer the problem; mediocrity is the issue. Calling the assumptions on which federal programs had been based "outdated," Finn argues for new federal policy for the twenty-first century that would be essentially laissez-faire. He also emphasizes that current federal policy, based on past federal educational policy, "may do more harm than good."

Other supporters of charter schools, such as Paul Hill, argue that federal programs only affect schools negatively and must be changed (Hill 2000).

As Finn writes:

> An immense bureaucracy has developed and must be sustained by con-
> tinuous infusions of federal funds. It isn't only federal employees, but also
> extensive colonies of federal program administrators in state and local ed-
> ucation agencies that absorb dollars. Too much money goes to underwrite
> administrators and middlemen rather than to educate children. . . . On the
> whole, today's federal elementary-secondary programs have not achieved
> their own goals. Worse, they do not even take aim at the main problems
> facing schools today, while managing to get in the way of those who try to
> reform schools. (Kanstoroom and Finn 1999)

The solution, Finn and his colleagues contend (Kanstoroom and Finn
1999), is a complete overhaul of federal educational policy for the
twenty-first century, one that abolishes past bureaucratic procedures
and entrusts states with federal dollars—without rules or regulations to
demonstrate compliance. States, Finn argues, can make the best educational decisions with federal funds dependent on the needs of residents
in their states.

With a centrist presidency in place during the 1990s, this philosophy
flourished. Millions of dollars were allocated on an increasing basis to
charter schools, based on a widespread belief that the public educational system as it existed was broken and a promising new alternative
based on free market forces needed to be in place as a type of repair.
State legislatures followed suit, passing enabling charter schools legislation in the majority of states, although charter school advocates do not
consider all legislation equally "strong."

When Bush assumed the presidency in 2001, he had a charge from
conservatives and from education reformers intent on improving the
nation's schools. The imperative to serve high-poverty schools was
placed high on his legislative agenda (No Child Left Behind), as were
charter schools, with an additional $175 million slated for a special char-
ter schools fund, in addition to the approximately $180 million per year
spent in federal support of charter schools.

At the beginning of the twenty-first century, the essentials were in
place for charter schools to flourish and expand. The nation already had
experienced sorting, tracking, and the developing of a wide array of educational alternatives. With charter schools, an odd hybrid of public dol-

lars, private values, and "alternatives" within the mainstream public educational system, one conclusion loomed: charter schools were not a historical accident, but an inevitability. In chapter 3, I discuss and analyze the sometimes turbulent and contradictory stream of state legislation that accompanied the growth of charter schools.

AN ANALYSIS OF CHARTER
SCHOOLS LEGISLATION

Charter schools come into being after state legislators and state boards of education decree their existence. Minnesota started the trend and it spread west quickly, captivating the interest of legislators in Arizona and California. Soon the novel idea spread across the country, pushed by advocates for change and critics of the status quo "government schools." Few legislatures started their examination of charter legislation from scratch. They borrowed concepts and phrases and even exact wording from one another. Special interests behind charters and those opposed to them pushed and shoved to influence the final wording state by state. After the first decade, the country was left with a potpourri of charter schools legislation. Enough difference exists from state to state to prevent easy generalizations about these laws. It is, however, possible to extract some key facts.

As the second charter schools decade opened, forty states had passed charter schools legislation (Maryland became the fortieth state in May 2003), plus Washington, D.C., and Puerto Rico. This legislation varies widely across states. In some states the laws that permit charter schools exist but are considered so troublesome that a charter school has not even opened its doors (Mississippi is one example). In others, the original legislation has come under scrutiny as the nation's fiscal crisis weighs heavily on state coffers and consequently the state's ability to support its public schools.

ADVOCATES RANK STATE LAWS

Special interests of all stripes refer to charter legislation as either "strong" or "weak." The educational establishment typically refers to a "weak" law as one that treats charters as a noble experiment and therefore caps the number that can be created. Such a law would also require the charter to be created only by a local school board that retains responsibility for its operation. A "strong" law, by this way of thinking, would be one that encourages multiple authorizers, unlimited numbers of charters, and maximum flexibility from local and state laws and regulations.

Undoubtedly the loudest voice on behalf of advocates is the Center for Education Reform (CER) out of Washington, D.C. This special-interest advocacy group sees charter schools as a preferable alternative to regular public schools and tends not to falter when promoting the former and condemning the latter. Its website ranking of strong and weak state laws is probably the best known and most often referenced. Even the U.S. Department of Education's website, at least when the Republicans are in charge, links to CER. Parenthetically, one might think the U.S. Department of Education's charter schools website would provide better or more current information, and it certainly can be consulted for other resources, but it relies on the CER for its statistics on charter schools across states. The CER has published a table at edreform.com/charter_schools/laws/ranking_chart.pdf that shows exactly what it means by strong and weak legislation.

The CER uses criteria that include the following:

- The year the law passed.
- The number of schools allowed.
- Whether multiple chartering authorities are permissible.
- How many charter applicants are eligible.
- How many new starts are allowed.
- Whether the school can be started without evidence of local support.

- Whether the legislation offers an automatic waiver from state and district laws.
- The extent of legal/operational autonomy.
- The extent of guaranteed full per-pupil funding.
- The extent of fiscal autonomy.
- Whether the legislation exempts charter schools from collective bargaining agreement/district work rules. (CER, January 2003)

The strong legislation, according to the CER, does several things. First and foremost, it releases charter schools—particularly newly created charter schools—from the same rules and regulations that regular public schools must follow (except in the case of federal entitlements). In doing so, it reinforces the argument frequently advanced by charter advocates that bureaucracy is part of the problem that burdens regular public education. "Release us from this burden," the argument goes, "and we will show you how well we can do." Therefore, charter advocacy groups like the CER promote "strong" legislation that is strong about autonomy for charter schools, strong about limitless numbers of charter schools that can operate in a state; strong about allowing the lengthiest charters possible before the school must reapply for continued status; and strong about granting more autonomy to charter schools from the outset so that they are not held too accountable to their sponsoring agencies or authorizers.

The weak legislation, charter school advocates would contend, puts restrictions on charter schools. It may cap the number of charter schools per state and submit them to reporting guidelines that charter school advocates would argue are the antithesis of the deregulation that the movement requires in order to succeed. Or it may demand a stronger relationship between the charter school and the authorizer. Conversion charter schools are considered weak in general because they exist in the same public school district in which they were housed to start with and therefore are subject to school board regulations and rules.

Charter school advocates need and want strong laws so that their schools can spread without regulatory checks or caps. They crave autonomy from regulation and, of course, promise heightened accountability in return.

What is fascinating to observe, as the next decade of charter schools unfolds, is the impact of the No Child Left Behind (NCLB) legislation on charter schools in states that previously enjoyed strong legislation or pro-charter legislation. Even charter schools in states that enjoyed almost unprecedented autonomy and growth, such as Arizona with its fifteen-year term for an initial charter, now will experience a press for both high-quality teachers and higher student outcomes. This press may do two things: (1) result in the closing of a charter school entirely, after it has endured the humiliation of being labeled "low performing," or (2) see charter schools turn into clones of the regular public schools they sought to flee. There is a third possibility that they may become receiving schools for students who are in existing low-performing schools but cannot find a school of choice that they want to attend. This situation could also overwhelm them into shutting their doors.

OTHER INFORMATIVE CRITERIA FOR LEGISLATION

The Education Commission of the States (ECS) maintains a charter schools section on its website (www.ecs.org) as well and has published a variety of issues briefs on charter schools. These briefs are divided into categories that include charter schools finance, autonomy, teachers, and accountability. Each brief presents a table in which a variety of questions about the state's legislation are posed and answered.

The following are some sample questions that ECS asks:

- Does the state allow existing public schools to convert to charter schools?
- Does the state allow for the creation of start-up charter schools?
- Are charter schools part of the school district or legally independent?
- Does the state specify the charter schools or the students that must be given preference?
- Does the state have any caps on the number of charter schools?
- Who can approve charter schools?
- Does the state require charter schools to submit annual reports?
- Does the state list grounds for terminating a school's charter? (ECS, April 2003)

These syntheses of informative facts lead to the overarching question: To what extent do the existing laws meet the needs of charter school authorizers and prospective operators? And to what extent do they match the rhetoric that charter school operators advance to further their cause?

WILL CHARTER SCHOOLS BECOME ACCOUNTABLE FOR STUDENT OUTCOMES?

Although it appears that a shift in the legislation is on its way for the next decade, certain patterns can be discerned from the past decade of state charter schools legislation. In states ranked strong by CER, the majority of states specify in their legislation that charter schools should meet the state's accountability provisions. While this may seem outdated in a time of NCLB, it is noteworthy because a number of states that are *not* identified as having strong charter legislation by the CER do not make the same commitment, raising the question: Why are these labeled strong and not weak? Is accountability not a hallmark of the charter schools movement?

Not surprisingly, increased accountability for improved student achievement outcomes is not specified in most states' charter schools legislation. In fact, few states demand any demonstration of *increased* accountability for charter school students, and some states excuse charter school students from taking mandatory state achievement tests.

Why is this not surprising? While state departments of education may join the rhetoric that clamors for heightened accountability, they are part of the education cartel that consists of universities and educational associations, all mutually reinforcing powerhouses. These powerful groups, including state boards and state departments of education, have demonstrated little interest in making time to run herd on schools created by parents and zealots. The state bureaucracies seem content to simply warn consumers that they ought to investigate charter schools carefully before enrolling their children in them. At the same time, these bureaucrats turn to legislators and soothe their concerns by saying the "marketplace" is the best way to judge the success or failure of a charter. That is, if the charter has a waiting list of student applicants, it must be doing something right. Conversely, if the charter school's enrollment dries up, it probably deserves to go out of business.

With the passage of the NCLB Act, charter schools run the same risk as their "nonindependent" public peers of being exposed as failing or low-performing schools. This ups the ante considerably for their considerations of accountability, but the federal legislation—while pro-choice—robs them of a considerable amount of their deregulation.

The NCLB legislation is quite specific and introduces a regulatory specter to states:

> The accountability and testing provisions in *No Child Left Behind* must also be applied to charter schools in accordance with states' charter school laws. As public schools, charter schools are subject to the same accountability and testing requirements, but state-authorized chartering agencies, as established by state law, are responsible for ensuring charter schools are meeting the requirements and being held accountable. (U.S. Department of Education)

What are charter schools generally held to by state legislation when accountability for student outcomes is at issue? The Delaware law (rated strong by the CER) is fairly typical:

> The school has set goals for student performance and will utilize *satisfactory* indicators to determine whether its students meet or exceed such goals and the academic standards set by the State. The indicators shall include the assessments required for students in other public schools, although the charter school may adopt additional performance standards or assessment requirements, and shall include timelines for the achievement of student performance goals and the assessment of such performance. . . . The school proposes a *satisfactory* plan for evaluating student performance and procedures for taking corrective action in the event that student performance at the charter school falls below such standards which are *reasonably* likely to succeed [italics mine]. (U.S. Department of Education 2001)

There are other implications. This lack of information influences the evaluation and selection of instructional staff. If a majority of students score at higher levels than students at public noncharter schools, when other factors are controlled, it could indicate that the teaching staff is doing a better-than-average job. The converse is also true. Just as a lack of reliable information about student performance can influence the choice of staff, it can influence decisions about innovations, reforms, and instructional approaches—even the choice of classroom materials.

DEREGULATION AND AUTONOMY: WHERE DO CHARTERS STAND?

Does the charter schools legislation reveal that charter schools have achieved the desired degree of deregulation from the rules and regulations that govern other public schools? To what extent is the importance of deregulation and autonomy—while at the same time operating under the constraints that must be in place for public schools that receive federal funds—specified in the existing charter schools legislation?

The facts are mixed. Regarding the CER's strong laws, it is apparent that charter school advocates concur that in order to be strong, a majority of schools must be required to hire a certain percentage of certified instructional staff. But they also rank other states as having strong pieces of legislation that do *not* require hiring certified teachers or instructional staff. Clearly, the requirements that charter schools be able to demonstrate they have certified instructional staff—an issue near and dear to most parents—are not considered all that important by the CER.

This is a bit of a puzzle. And it suggests a lesser degree of deregulation than most charter schools would like. The fact that most charter schools are not required to hire *all* certified instructional staff frees them both from a financial concern and from the "step" progression familiar to most public, noncharter school employees. They also could hire content experts or other individuals known for their achievements who do not have licensure as teachers.

On the positive side, this might match a school's desire for innovation in pedagogy. The negative side of this equation, of course, is that uncertified teachers may have little knowledge of schools or students; they simply might be seeking a temporary "professional" job with little commitment to teaching or to education.

There are also a variety of reports and studies that point to the fact that relatively inexperienced teachers gravitate to charter schools, probably because more seasoned teachers are reluctant to give up their place in a public school and their position on the career ladder in terms of salary (U.S. Department of Education 2001). And the U.S. Department of Education, in the age of NCLB, is adamant about "high-quality teachers" in every classroom by the beginning of the 2005–2006 school year—including in charter schools.

Will these teachers, and perhaps also principals attracted by less regulation, flee more-regulated charter schools and return to regular public schools—particularly those that are not as high needs or demanding? Or will they choose to stay the course? These are issues that seem relevant as NCLB increases its regulatory hold on public education.

CONCLUSION

At the beginning of the second charter decade, the financial plight having an impact on all fifty states is forcing some politicians to reconsider their charter legislation. The public school people are making a strong and plausible case that charter schools are draining critical resources out of regular schools at a time of severe funding cutbacks. At the same time, the NCLB legislation is significantly affecting charter schools. Their advocates are going to be assaulting the state politicians for exemptions from intrusive federal policies.

All these forces will lead to even more flux in the state legislation over the second decade of charter schools. This result raises interesting speculations about what degree of freedom or autonomy charter schools might experience in their next decade, what caliber of staff they are likely to recruit and retain, and what will happen to their student enrollment if these so-called reform schools increasingly resemble regular public schools.

4

CHARTERING ENTIRE DISTRICTS

When public school critics of charter schools complain about these interlopers, someone always says, "We ought to make every school a charter school. We ought to charter the entire district!" Well, why not? With one sweeping stroke, districts could be empowered to enjoy the freedoms and opportunities of many newly created charter schools.

Charter schools, of course, are a completely different entity than charter districts. A district obtains a charter for itself to change its relationship with the state. A school obtains a charter for itself to change its relationship with its district or authorizing agency, as well as the state. Advocates for both argue they want to decrease regulation to increase innovation.

But charter districts are cramped by faulty legislation and currently seem to offer little more than a time-consuming, resource-burning distraction for well-intentioned superintendents. Those who crave release from state regulations may engage in a long battle to secure freedoms from the state—but not enough—and they are clearly insufficient to ensure impressive gains in either school culture building or student achievement.

The following facts about charter districts illustrate the painful restrictions of this movement:

- Eight charter districts exist in merely three states—far from a trend.
- One state authorized a charter district that decided to revert to its original status at the end of its charter.
- Charter district expansion has been curbed by burdensome applications processes and loopholes in state laws (including caps on total numbers of charter districts per state).
- Charter district administrators admit that most improvements realized under the charter could have occurred without it.

The token nature of this reform—along with its stunted potential—is poignantly apparent in the words of one superintendent of a charter district: "We are not doing anything revolutionary—but think of what we could do." The good intentions and imagination that motivated the charter district movement are not sufficient to ensure its success. While school administrators could be invigorated professionally by the notion of freedom from regulation, current legislation will curb their best efforts and stymie their plans for broadscale school improvement.

THE ISSUE: POTENTIAL IMPACT AND VALUE OF CHARTER DISTRICTS

At first glance, charter districts seem to offer an inventive way to conduct the business of schooling. Ingenious structural and governance arrangements for existing schools could be built—along with refashioned district and school relationships. Change could occur rapidly, unencumbered by the grinding pace of a bureaucracy and a tedious, school-by-school approach to reform. Creating charter districts seems to be a natural for school system leaders.

While charter schools extend a new, but relatively small, building-focused alternative to educational consumers, charter districts have the potential to free public education at a much larger level—and with a strikingly comprehensive scope. School administrators who struggle with burdensome regulations imposed by states and unions may want to charter their entire districts in the hope that this new status could create or facilitate the following:

- the proper climate for reform as a districtwide regulatory burden is lifted;
- freedom from many state rules and regulations that stifle reform efforts;
- allocation of resources with less state-imposed restriction on specific funds (monies go where the district wants them to go);
- district control over instructional methods and choice of materials, rather than state-mandated methods and texts.

And in return, unlike charter schools, charter districts are not threatened with a complete shutdown if they do not perform to standards stipulated in the charter. The maximum penalty a charter district could experience is the revocation of the charter or a return to the previous status as a public school district that must comply with all state rules and regulations.

WHAT ARE CHARTER DISTRICTS?

A charter district comes into being when a district wants to leverage a shift in its relationship with the state and when state legislation permits such a rearrangement. As superintendents seek charter district status, the legislation usually forces them to campaign for wide buy-in and involvement from a variety of constituent groups. But the campaign, sadly enough, is not one of substance—nor can it be—given the restrictive legislation.

Some charter districts also have charter schools within their boundaries. In Georgia, for example, where one district became a charter district and then converted back to noncharter status at the end of its charter, charter status was obtained for the district by converting each school to charter status under existing state legislation. But we discovered that most charter districts are not districts in which all schools are charter schools. This troubles some charter school advocates, who seek a fundamental redefinition of the relationship between the individual school and the district. To these advocates, chartering entire districts with the aim of shifting relationships with the state begs the question—and avoids the ideology—of the charter schools movement. In fact, the reasons districts seek charter status vary, as do their student demographics and motives for broadscale change. For example, a district in Pennsylvania and another in Michigan are sometimes referred to as charter districts. These districts are both managed by private, for-profit management companies.

The Pennsylvania district was taken over by the state; it contracted with three for-profit management companies to inject choice into the system and turn around a persistent culture of failure. But state department of education personnel in Pennsylvania quickly clarify that this district is not a charter district.

The Michigan district had no recourse if it wanted to stay in operation. It had a huge deficit, combined with dismal student achievement; declining enrollments drained by area charter schools; and a state that did not want to take it over. The district's only choice was to contract with a for-profit management company in exchange for paying off the deficit. This Faustian bargain runs contrary to the notion of a district freely choosing how it wants to manage its business, its instruction, and its selection of materials. In this case, a private for-profit company made all such decisions for the district—which had little choice after exploring other options, including annexation to neighboring districts. Furthermore, the Michigan superintendent was baffled by the description of her district as a charter district. When interviewed for this book, she said, "We have to abide by all state rules and regulations and are monitored just like other public school districts in the state."

CHARTER DISTRICTS: THE ADMINISTRATORS SPEAK

What do superintendents in charter districts relate about their experiences? In this section, we summarize their experiences. The districts we selected were chosen to showcase geographic spread as well as demographic and ideological differences. Administrators were interviewed by phone with a uniform protocol of questions.

California: Small Size, Conservative Values

California is home to five of the nation's charter districts, all of them small and rural. Three of the charter districts reside in the same county district, close to Fresno. Agrarian work and conservative values permeate all five districts.

The Kingsburg Elementary School District in Kingsburg, California, received charter status in 1996 after a principal and its superintendent at the time invested themselves in the concept. As enthusiasm grew, teachers shared the idea with parents and met with a positive reception. Mark Ford, the current superintendent, has worked in the district for most of the years of implementation. But other factors played into the mix of administrator and teacher-driven change. The state endorsed a whole-language approach, which met with the opposition of teachers and parents in the district. Following a long series of public disgruntlements with state mandates, the district and community rebelled.

Teachers believed other instructional approaches were preferable; parents agreed. They resented a departure from the basal reader of their own youths and viewed its imposition by the state as an additional irritant. As a result, the parents in this district were galvanized to support chartering the entire district in order to free it from the state regulatory code.

Ford views charter district status as an enormous mine of limitless potential to be tapped. While admitting to little innovation in his district in terms of pedagogical practices that have resulted from gaining charter status, the fact that approximately 60–70 percent of his students perform at grade level may be because of the district choosing its own curriculum and methods. In particular, Ford points to a music program, a K–3 reading program, and a grades 5 and 6 science curriculum that has been built independently of state textbook adoptions.

Schools in this all-elementary district are divided by grade level, but that is not a shift since gaining charter status. In an unusual departure from typical grade groupings, one school serves K–2, another 3–4, yet another 5–6, and another 7–8. As a result, students develop close relationships with their peers and with teachers. They move together through the school sequence and attend high school together in another district. Ford describes his community as "entrenched in tradition." He adds, "Some teachers are teaching the grandchildren of students they taught in the past."

Conservative values, including an emphasis on strong local control, have permeated the district's philosophy that it should make its own decisions about how monies are spent and what textbooks students should use. Building principals have control over hiring and firing, in co-operation with the central office, and do not contend with unions. "Never have had one, and never will," Ford says emphatically.

With two thousand students, this district has the dual advantage of close ties between students, teachers, and parents—and small size and safety. Approximately 47 percent of its students are white; another 47 percent Hispanic; and tiny percentages of blacks, Asians, and a growing population of Sikh students dot the otherwise dominantly Hispanic and white demographics of the district.

The superintendent who led the move to charter district status had to fight a number of legal battles to ensure that the district secured it. As Ford says laconically, "California law did not forbid districts to go char-ter, but it didn't encourage it either." Ford believes that charter district status means freedom from regulation and speed. "You just move," he emphasizes, "you don't wait." But the ability to move rapidly has not brought about startling curricular or pedagogical innovations—although the district can point to changes.

But the overall business of educating students in this all-charter district does not proceed much differently than it did in the past. The biggest ad-justment for the Kingsburg district has been expanding the boundaries of imagination to fit new and spacious parameters of possibility. "I always use the example of a racehorse that is taken out of its paddock to run a race," he says. "The horse runs a good race under the hand of the jockey and re-turns to its small paddock. But when you take the same horse out to fifty acres of grass and expect it to run free, it may not move very far, doesn't realize how much room it actually has." This unexplored territory, Ford says, is a sad reminder that districts may succeed in their efforts to gain charter status but fail to examine and fulfill their many options.

In another small elementary charter district in Hanford, California, the superintendent holds a different view. Its only school (a charter school) constitutes the Delta View Joint Union Elementary District—a type of charter egg encased in a charter shell. Charter district status (again, for the one charter school) was advanced by a group of parents in tandem with the previous superintendent who believed they could impose tighter academic standards if the district, which is highly rural and agrarian, had charter status.

Dale Campbell, the superintendent, is candid about what selectivity meant to that group of parents. The district has a 75 percent free and reduced lunch population and is 60 percent Hispanic. Parents who were eager for charter district status tended, he notes, to be longtime residents. "These parents felt there would be more buy-in if all parents had to sign a compact with the district," Campbell says. "We had traditional boundaries, but since charter status goes beyond those boundaries, we would have the ability to send students elsewhere."

Key components of the parent/district compact included the requirement that students attend school at least 95 percent of all school days and complete all homework—a move to higher standards. But the compact is essentially toothless: There are no sanctions for parents who do not comply with the compact, Campbell notes. Currently, the district enjoys 96 percent attendance with "most students handing in their work," according to Campbell. A few students have opted out of the district and attend neighboring districts, either because of a personality conflict with a teacher or because it is not "a good match," although Campbell emphasizes that neighboring districts have a reciprocal approach.

Campbell is not optimistic about the future of charter districts, except in the case of small districts. He points to a tightening of the standards for charter schools and charter districts in California, which he views as a positive development. "Financially, we are in the same shape as before," he explains. "We have a little more latitude with staff, because we can hire part-time teachers without certification." These new hiring practices are not confounded by the presence of a union because the district does not have one.

While charter district status might carry a certain cachet, Campbell predicts it will be difficult for large districts to move to charter status because of the requirements of the legislation in their individual states. In California, for example, the votes of at least 50 percent of teachers in the district are required before the state will consider an application for charter status. Rather than more charter districts, Campbell believes there will be an increase in individual charter schools. He says that charter districts are "good PR" and he would want to maintain his own district status, but he has mixed feelings about whether he would encourage other superintendents to strive for the same status for their districts.

"Charter districts can be a tool, because of the buy-in from parents and their commitment to higher attendance standards," he says.

California's charter schools legislation includes only a paragraph pertinent to charter districts. The five small charter districts in California seized this paragraph and applied for charter district status. However, 50 percent of the teachers within the district must sign the charter petition; the petition must contain all the elements specified under California law for charter schools; the proposed charter districts must specify alternative public school attendance arrangements for pupils residing within the school district who choose not to attend charter schools; and the districtwide charter petition must be approved by joint action of the Superintendent of Public Instruction and the State Board of Education (California Charter Schools Act of 1992). Charters may not exceed five years, although they can be renewed for periods of five years.

Florida: Broad Strokes, New Relationships

By way of contrast, two of Florida's large districts have crafted a different relationship with the state—but the freedoms they enjoy are not open to all districts in the state. The School District of Hillsborough County, one of Florida's large charter districts, has 168,000 students and approximately 23,000 employees. The district ranges from a very urban to a vast suburban population to a rural, agriculturally dominated population. The fastest-growing population is Hispanic, at approximately 21.5 percent, with a white population of 50 percent, a black population of 24 percent, and the remaining population a wide range of different nationalities. This latter population has a pronounced need for English language services.

Its assistant superintendent for instruction, Donnie Evans, says there were three main reasons the district sought and gained charter status. The first, he says, was tied directly to the desire to improve the performance of students and schools. "We wanted to find ways to think outside the box," he notes. "Obstacles in our state statutes prevented us from doing that. We wanted waivers, but prior to the time when districts could gain charter status in our state, each waiver had to be requested on a statute-by-statute basis." This cumbersome way of seeking freedom from regulation, he adds, made charter district status additionally appealing. "We also wanted to have the freedom that charter schools have," Evans observes, "their flexibility."

And finally, he adds that part of the move to charter district status had little to do with statutes but a great deal to do with paradigms. "History limits us," he says. "This can be a very big problem, getting away from the type of thinking that believes that things must be done the same way just because they always have been done that way." The district's new freedom can be seen in modest examples of course-taking flexibility previously prohibited by Florida state statutes. "We wanted to connect with kids at risk," Evans emphasizes, "and we felt the statutes limited that."

While the district has a strong teacher union, it is now exploring alternative certification and has been freed to do so under its charter status. Evans emphasizes that the planning team that worked on the district's application for charter status was carefully composed to include representatives from unions, the business community, instructional staff, local universities, and administrators—to ensure maximum buy-in and minimal conflict. Their groups appointed these individuals. Principals' councils at each level—elementary, middle, and high school—appointed individual representatives, as did the teachers' union and another collective bargaining unit.

Changing the district's relationship with the state was the primary thrust of the team's work from the beginning, Evans observes. "We are working now in both finances and human resources to get more authority for each to the principals," he adds. While principals have the authority to hire staff after a district human resources screening, he would like to see principals with additional authority over their budgeting. This, he believes, can be accomplished with the district's move to charter status. The biggest surprise, Evans says, was achieving charter district status, which he sees in some ways as incompatible with traditionally held values. "This district is so traditional," he emphasizes, "that it was surprising we were able to do this."

But it is difficult to see what is particularly innovative in the district's current practices or what runs contrary to tradition except for the release from some state requirements. The district, despite its charter status, does not have open enrollment. Recent court decisions have led it to unitary status as a school system or a plan to end court-ordered busing. As unitary status is phased in throughout the district, by 2004 a limited version of choice will be available to district students and their parents. Hillsborough County refers to this plan as "controlled choice," through which parents may choose a school within their region or zone, but assignment is controlled by available space.

Why are more districts not moving to charter status? Evans believes that traditional patterns of behavior and beliefs inhibit more districts from taking such action. "People are hesitant to challenge traditions," he says, "and it may be that charter districts are considered an offshoot of charter schools. There are a lot of people who are not supportive of charter schools." Evans also believes that several districts will apply for charter status, primarily to change their relationships with the state—but the number of total charter districts permissible under Florida law is six. As for its innovative qualities, he believes charter district status has considerable potential. "We don't have an excuse anymore not to perform," he says. "For that reason, it has the potential to outweigh any effort in this district."

Florida law allows charter school districts to apply for exemptions from state statutes except for those that deal with the election of school boards, teacher unions, public meetings and records, financial disclosure, conflict of interest, and "sunshine" laws (those laws that govern open meetings). In return, charter districts must establish performance goals, assessment measures for those goals, and a time frame to meet performance goals.

Georgia: A Five-Year Plan, Then Business as Usual

In Georgia, the Cartersville City School System in Cartersville has had a different experience: five years as a charter district followed by a return to regular district status. Superintendent Mike Bryans describes his district as one that serves approximately 3,600 students with a previously high track record of academic achievement. The district's demographics include a growing Hispanic population of approximately 11 percent, with an additional 28 percent classified loosely as "minority."

Cartersville City wanted more funds from the state; it also did not want to mandate an instructional approach or method from the central office. As the district sought charter status, each school wrote individual charters for their own relationships with the district. In essence, rather than fight a battle for charter district legislation, the district used existing state charter schools legislation to gain charter district status.

While each school was unique, according to Bryans, there were common themes: increased parental involvement, along with leadership and maximum buy-in from all stakeholders. Another benefit, he adds, was a clear articulation of what the district wanted to accomplish within five years.

Basic changes included scheduling shifts and a restructuring at the elementary level to allow small-group instruction. To accomplish this, other classes increased their size—classes such as art and music. Reading groups with a maximum of twelve students were constructed, along with eighty different levels of proficiency. With additional funds that the district received from the state as a consequence of becoming a charter district, staff development monies were allocated to train teachers in the method they wanted: direct instruction.

Bryans emphasizes that teachers wanted to move to a direct instruction approach, describing it as "very scripted with lots of structure." Could this shift to direct instruction have been accomplished without charter district status? "Certainly," he concedes, "and we could have accomplished lots of goals without the charter."

As the years of the five-year charter progressed, the state of Georgia moved to embrace some of the changes the district had instituted as part of its charter. School councils, for example, once innovative, now are state-mandated. Bryans emphasizes that when the district had charter status, "We looked the same. We smelled the same. But we continued to see improvement, perhaps two to three percentile points on standardized tests." Apart from the injection of state funds the Cartersville City district received, Bryans describes the benefits of charter status as political. "The beauty of it," he says, "is that we didn't have to mandate anything—it all came from our staff."

New Mexico: A Lonely Struggle for Reforms

The sole charter district in New Mexico, Rio Rancho Public Schools, has fought a long battle to gain charter status. A relatively young district, it has been in existence for seven years—and once was suffused with deep citizen dissatisfaction with public schools. A suburban system of fifty thousand people, this district, according to its superintendent, Sue Cleveland, "was born in revolution." For example, a substantial (35 percent) Hispanic population was adamant about implementing more successful methods to the bilingual education approach, with parents lining up to demand new assessment models and alternatives for their children. A relatively small, fluctuating population of Native American students (3–7 percent) and a correspondingly fluctuating population of black students (3–7 percent) also provide diversity. The remainder of the student population is Anglo.

In this fast-growing community, Cleveland was frustrated by the inflexible state regulations that made it increasingly difficult for the district to realize its goals. Intrigued with charter district status, she became a key part of the effort to influence and encourage the creation of legislation that would permit districts to move to charter status. "We felt very constrained by the state," Cleveland explains. "And some state department officials fought us very hard as we moved to chartering the district. The state board, on the other hand, sensed the need for changes and were willing to give us this opportunity."

The application process was arduous, culminating in a municipal election. In addition, it was necessary to achieve a two-thirds affirmative union-supervised vote. "We ran the election," she says, "like a bond campaign. We have a four-and-a-half-year charter but we must return to the state board in two years to report on progress."

While charter status might appear to offer this district considerable latitude, the superintendent describes it as a hard-won process of tough negotiations. "We didn't get the flexibility from the state that we really wanted," she notes. "We negotiated with the state department every step of the way, but we certainly did not get everything we felt we needed—and in some cases, needed desperately."

The biggest positive change, Cleveland reports, is psychological. "Staff feel we are not doing business as usual. We have greater responsibility to solve our own problems but we have more flexibility than before." She describes previous efforts to work with the state as a catch-22. "The State Department of Education would identify outcomes, specify materials, specify methods, and in some cases, would establish financial constraints. But when the outcome wasn't very good, they would ask what the district was doing wrong." Cleveland emphasizes a key point. "When you allow people to use their best judgment, only then can you hold people accountable."

This district has open enrollment as required by New Mexico, with waiting lists of students at every school. However, this has resulted in some local hostility. "Parents resent people who don't pay taxes here and enroll their children in our district," she acknowledges. "And sometimes families come here when their children have been in serious trouble somewhere else." Part of the open enrollment process includes blanket permission to teachers to enroll their children, regardless of where teachers live. "A lot of residents don't like that," the superintendent adds, "but obtaining and retaining good staff is critical to our efforts."

Site-based management exists, but not at the most far-reaching levels. "Principals can hire staff, within union constraints, but some financial decisions are limited because of scarce funding and regulatory constraints," she says. The biggest surprise, Cleveland reports, was the polarization that developed, the extremes in emotions about the proposed charter. "Some people saw a nefarious plot," she says. "On the other hand, the business community was strongly in favor of the charter."

She also points to heightened accountability for the district. "We have to report on our progress more frequently than any other district in the state. We have had significant successes in improving student achievement but obviously we won't abandon what has brought us success before." Major changes on the agenda include a hard look at bilingual education and how well it serves the needs of the students. "We are rebuilding our bilingual programs," Cleveland says.

But could the district have made these changes without becoming a charter district? "Yes, but it would have been slower," she says. "We now have total control of our instructional materials, some financial flexibility, and more control over the school-day structure. We see enormous promise in this movement, more so than charter schools that seem dependent on the individual school leader and the parents to provide a direction for the school." She adds, "A charter district is different. When districts are well run, fewer charter schools may need to develop. When districts are well run, they provide services and support to their administrators and teachers so they can do their work and focus on their main task of teaching and learning."

She ponders one question. "Why give all this wonderful freedom to a charter school and not to a charter district? If we can make a difference at the school level, think what differences we can make at the district level." As a superintendent, Cleveland admits that she is reform oriented. "I will get there without it," she concludes, "but charter status is a tool that facilitates this process." Yet New Mexico's legislation is far from encouraging. Only three "pilot" charter districts are permitted by state law: large, medium, and small, respectively.

New Mexico's application process would discourage all but the hardiest superintendents. The local school board first applies for a charter to the state board. As is typical of charter schools, this application must include the mission of the proposed district, the evidence that the charter is educationally and economically sound, an explanation of new relationships between personnel and the district, and a list of waivers requested from state board rules. If the local and state boards approve the application, the district then must hold a municipal election, posing the question of charter district status to the community. A majority vote must be gained. In addition, 65 percent of school district employees must sign a petition in support of charter district status. If the election and petition are secured, the charter cannot exceed six calendar years—but Rio Rancho received only four calendar years. Department of education personnel visit the district "at least once each year" in an evaluative role. The charter can be revoked or the district placed on probationary status—although the district will not cease to operate.

Texas: Legislation, but No Charter Districts to Date

Texas has legislation that permits "home-rule school district charters," but this legislation is loaded with caveats. Probably as a consequence, there are no charter districts in Texas. The applications process is laborious. First, a district's school board appoints a charter commission for developing a charter if at least 5 percent of the registered voters of the district sign a petition for that purpose. In addition, at least two-thirds of the board's members must adopt a resolution ordering the appointment of a charter commission.

If those conditions are met, fifteen district residents are appointed to the commission to reflect the racial, ethnic, socioeconomic, and geographic diversity of the district. A majority of the fifteen residents must be parents of school-age children attending the district's public schools. And at least 25 percent must be classroom teachers selected by the representatives of the professional staff (unions). The charter must meet the specifications of the state legislation, which are typical of requirements of prospective charter schools. On completion, the charter commission submits the proposed charter to the secretary of state, who determines if the proposed charter changes the governance of the school district.

If it does, the secretary of state notifies the school board in the district, which must submit the proposed change to the United States Department of Justice or the United States District Court for the District of Columbia for preclearance under the Voting Rights Act. The charter commission also submits the proposed charter to the commissioner for legal review. Modifications, if any, are suggested and the charter is changed to reflect these recommendations. If the commissioner does not act within the prescribed time frame, the charter is approved. But the process does not end there. After the home-rule school district charter is approved, the district's school board must order an election on the proposed charter. Tight regulations govern this election. For the charter to be approved, a majority of the voters of the district must vote in favor of it. Moreover, the election is ineffectual unless at least 25 percent of the district's registered voters vote in whatever election has the adoption of the charter on the ballot.

Almost any superintendent would hesitate before embarking on such a laborious process. In its efforts to avoid bureaucratic rules and regulations, the very process of applying for release from such regulation seems to involve more trouble than the freedom may be worth. A superintendent's time conceivably could be devoted to the process of shepherding the district through approval, which is not ensured and may net only modest autonomy if granted.

THE EVIDENCE: CHARTER DISTRICTS AND THE WORLD OF SCHOOL ADMINISTRATION, TEACHING, AND LEARNING

Key threads run through widely differing districts. These strands, which we will summarize in this section, can be described as

- the weight of tradition;
- conservative, parent-held values;
- a desire for the appearance of change;
- a need for politically safe reform;
- restrictive legislation that negates the concept that underpins charter districts and ensures their failure.

We noted that most superintendents spoke of the bonds of tradition that permeated their very different communities and districts. From a rebellious small district in California that fought state control to a huge Florida district with sprawling borders and dizzying student diversity, superintendents emphasized the need to overcome tradition and do something new.

Yet are charter districts innovative? Are they truly something new? Or are they something comfortable that appeases conservative values and a desire to legitimize the status quo? While these districts enjoy some freedoms from state rules and regulations, in most states these releases could be obtained through an admittedly painstaking process of applying for waivers. In actuality, charter districts appear to be a strange hybrid of tradition grafted onto conservative values and parental hostility toward public education—all components that have been tapped into successfully by advocates of charter schools.

Another irony about charter districts is inherent in superintendents' battles with tradition to find something new. In reality, when superintendents spoke about battling tradition, they found their strongest support for chartering their districts in the roots of traditional beliefs and values in their districts. Charter district status became a politically adroit way to honor stakeholders, to include them in some kind of decision-making process (although not as substantive as a districtwide reform endeavor), and to respect their input.

Parents, similarly, were charged with signing compacts and charters for new roles and responsibilities with the districts in which their children attended school. Yet in most cases, these compacts lacked credibility and could be violated at any time. Again, there is a "feel good" aspect to this type of parental involvement—an initial rush of goodwill toward the district's "new" campaign, followed by the detritus of waning enthusiasm once the meeting schedule loses its intensity.

Thus, parents, PTA members, union presidents (if applicable), and other constituents all have the opportunity to *feel* that something massive has been accomplished—when in reality, as superintendents admitted, any reform under consideration could have occurred without charter district status. The biggest benefit to charter school districts, we concluded, is the opportunity they offer to a wide array of constituents to express their points of view, buy into a change process, and enjoy the emotions that accompany the thrill of "being innovative." However, there is a "pick your battles" approach to this issue.

Superintendents interested in charter district status need to evaluate carefully whether they should advocate for legislation that will allow charter districts to thrive—or whether they want to seek charter status if legislation in their states permits charter districts. Either decision could be expensive in terms of resources expended for benefits gained.

If superintendents decide to advocate for legislation that would permit charter districts a broader scope with considerable autonomy, there are no good models of such legislation. Legislation that would permit charter districts to expand and thrive awaits development. Do superintendents want to invest themselves in the development of this legislation—or is their valuable time best spent in other endeavors? Also, if superintendents decide chartering their districts is possible under state law, they should ask themselves what they intend to accomplish after gaining the charter and if there is a shorter route that will allow them to accomplish the same goals. Should they spend precious resources trying to gain charter district status if the freedoms are largely symbolic or not sufficiently broad?

State legislation currently does not allow the relaxed freedoms this movement needs to flourish—even at the pilot level. Unless state policymakers take note, chartering entire districts will remain a largely symbolic action—one that superintendents might be well advised to avoid so they can invest their energies in actions that will pay greater dividends.

5

OBSTACLES AND BARRIERS

One of the hallmarks of the charter schools movement has been the numerous obstacles to the efforts of its advocates. Indeed, these problems have been considered severe enough that they could impede the movement's path to success as a full-scale, legitimate education reform that has exerted a broad impact on the lives of many students in the nation. The first step to success is *starting* a charter school from nothing or *converting* an existing school to charter status. The laws that govern these processes are variable between states, and negotiating them requires that pro-charter individuals and groups be nimble and, above all, knowledgeable of their state's legislation and the regulations that govern applications.

STARTING A CHARTER SCHOOL

In order to establish a charter school, its prospective operator or operators must secure the charter, or contract, that makes the school a legal entity in the state's public educational system and secures its public funds. The process of starting a charter school varies to some extent depending on the status of the school (newly created, conversion public, or a private school converting to charter school status) and the requirements of the legislation in the state that the charter school will be housed in. However, the application process is quite similar across states and across the different types of charter schools. Common components are required in virtually every state's legislation.

In many ways, the application for a charter resembles a grant application. Certain elements must be present; these are stipulated by state law. Different approaches to meeting the requirements of the application for a charter can be compared to the differences that groups of researchers might entertain about any educational topic under study and the various approaches they might choose to learn more about it.

In short, differences in charter school applications reflect the diversity of the constituents who want the school and whatever educational goals and outcomes they deem critical. Differences in authorizing agencies—such as state boards of education versus universities versus local school districts—also will affect the content and focus of an individual charter school's application.

TYPICAL APPLICATION COMPONENTS

The typical charter school application usually contains most or all the following components: a statement of the educational vision or mission; a statement of need or justification for the school; a description of the prospective educational program; specified learning objectives for students; how student assessment will be conducted; a financial plan that is accompanied by a three-to-five-year budget; a plan for governance; personnel policies (including collective bargaining, benefits, hiring, and dismissal procedures); admissions policies; information on the proposed facility (how it will be secured, whether it will be leased, and whether it is in compliance with safety regulations); provisions for insurance; compliance with state and federal regulations, as necessary; and discussion of how monitoring and evaluation of the school will be conducted (U.S. Department of Education 2003).

Application requirements from two different states, Massachusetts and Minnesota, illustrate what is typical. They also show the review and timeline to which applicants submit their applications for a charter.

Massachusetts allows two kinds of charter schools, "Commonwealth" school and "Horace Mann" schools. By law, Commonwealth charter schools are capped at 72, and Horace Mann schools at 48, for a total cap of 120. But the 2003 application materials make an important point: "In the 2002–2003 application cycle, there are 19 Commonwealth charters and 34 Horace Mann charters available." Clearly, conversion charter schools are more welcome in Massachusetts than are newly created charter schools.

The difference between the two types of charter schools in Massachusetts is simple: Commonwealth charter schools are *newly created* and their charters are granted by the state board of education, which also is the authorizer of Commonwealth schools. In addition, an independent board manages them. Horace Mann schools, in contrast, are converted public schools that have been approved by a local board and a bargaining agent, and then their charter is granted by the state board of education (U.S. Department of Education 2003). While neither Commonwealth nor Horace Mann schools are automatically exempt from state laws and regulations, they may apply for waivers from these regulations.

Most initial charters have a maximum term of five years, and charter school students must meet the same performance standards as other public school students. Massachusetts is a good example of a state in which charter schools are held closely to similar rigorous regulations as are regular public schools.

The review process in Massachusetts typically begins with a letter of intent, followed two weeks later with a prospectus no longer than ten pages. Within another month, the State Department of Education informs all applicants of their status; that is, if they have been selected to submit a final application, which is due a month later. Within another month, each application is evaluated, public hearings are held, superintendents in the districts in which the charter schools will be housed submit written reviews, interviews by department of education staff are conducted, the commissioner of education makes a recommendation, and finally the board of education votes on the charters to be granted.

The key elements in the Massachusetts application are mission, statement of need, the educational program, accountability, and governance and capacity. However, the commentary the State Department of Education offers prospective applicants to help with their applications is noteworthy. Under "accountability," the criteria are the following:

> Reviewers will look for a genuine and competent commitment to accountability for results, including a concrete description of the credible and multiple means the school would use to demonstrate the academic progress of its students. The application should describe compelling objectives that are consistent with its mission and program, as well as with high academic standards (U.S. Department of Education 2001).

Clearly, a wide range of responses could be considered acceptable concerning this important dimension of a charter school. The school has considerable latitude as it plans for this key component—a cornerstone of the charter schools movement.

PROBLEMS WITH THE APPLICATION PROCESS

The state's relatively rapid review process does not lend itself to more than the superficial. Within the relatively brief period of two months, charter school applications are submitted, written responses and reviews are secured, public hearings are held, and interviews of key respondents are conducted.

The length of time that prospective charter school operators have to go through the review process is rushed as well—again, much like a typical grant application cycle. One could argue that prospective operators should know every angle of the planned charter school inside and out, but this is unrealistic. It is far more common, as is frequently the case with grant applications, to write what seems appropriate or possible at the time and deal with the "problems" if charter status is granted.

Therein lies one of the largest problems. The brevity of planning time, even with planning grants from the U.S. Department of Education targeted especially for that purpose, can lead to a school that must be "up and running" in months, with staff hired, a principal in place, a core mission and values, and a curriculum that parents will endorse.

Minnesota's application process does not differ significantly from Massachusetts's, although this state is more visibly "pro-charter." The only apparent difference is the requirement that charter schools must use a nationally norm-referenced test for two academic areas. Its requirements for accountability include

> the specific and measurable outcomes pupils are expected to achieve in two academic areas and two non-academic areas related to the stated goals of the school. The academic outcomes must be assessed using a nationally norm referenced [*sic*] test. . . . Each school must determine the appropriate outcomes and means of measure that best reflects their curriculum. (U.S. Department of Education 2003)

A LACK OF RIGOR IN THE APPLICATION PROCESS

Neither application, in fact, appears particularly rigorous. Perhaps the most important criterion in both states is the quality of the budget for the length of the charter. While pragmatic, this runs contrary to the rhetoric of the charter schools movement about innovative educational practices that cannot be realized within the structure of conventional public schools as well as stringent accountability measures for student outcomes.

The actuality, of course, is that financial management has become one of the largest problems charter schools confront. Inexperienced charter school operators are suddenly confronted with a budget and a finite amount of money. Many charter schools have closed due to fiscal mismanagement, whether purposeful or not (U.S. Department of Education 2001).

THE REALITY OF RUNNING A CHARTER SCHOOL

Once chartered and in operation, what do most charter schools confront? The first set of obstacles is related to the daily functioning of a school: generating adequate revenue both to start the school and keep it in operation; allocation of resources; choice of curriculum and pedagogy; hiring, evaluation, and dismissal of staff; and overall strategic planning. Within these broad areas, myriad management issues confront the charter school operator who may be drawn ideologically to the challenge of the school as a reform enterprise and lack relevant experience in school finance, management, and school law.

Parenthetically, the problems reported by charter school operators seem to be improving to some degree. Since the genesis of the charter schools movement in the early 1990s, practical resources have been developed to help prospective charter school operators and their constituents plan the management, governance, fiscal operations, and other key aspects of the charter school (U.S. Department of Education 2001). Some states provide technical assistance upon request to start-up charter schools; federal monies are devoted to starting up charter schools; and all prospective charter school operators or interested educational stakeholders can follow guidebooks that advise them on key issues that range from budgeting to compliance with federal rules and regulations.

THE PROBLEMS: PRACTICAL, PREDICTABLE, AND PERNICIOUS

To a large extent, the problems reported by charter school operators are both practical and predictable. If charter schools are viewed as one powerful offshoot of the current reform movement, it becomes clear that their problems are shared by other public schools committed to a wide variety of school improvement efforts.

Certainly, none of the problems reported by charter school operators as most pressing are unknown to noncharter public schools engaged in reform. If considered in that context, the problems of charter schools are predictable, even unremarkable. They are practical because they revolve around the lifeblood of a school: revenue adequate to manage the educational program of the school, coupled with effective management of resources. Unfortunately, they become pernicious when they cannot be resolved.

What do charter school operators see as impediments to their efforts and to the charter schools movement as a whole? According to a four-year longitudinal federal study of charter schools that concluded in 2001, the top four reported problems among charter school operators were a lack of start-up funds, inadequate operating funds, a lack of planning time, and inadequate school facilities. These problems varied in severity, the fourth-year report concluded, depending on the type of charter school: newly created, preexisting public school, or preexisting private school (U.S. Department of Education 2001).

The study used self-reports of charter school operators to reach percentages based on the total number of charter schools in the nation who participated in the study. Overall, a lengthy array of problems was cited by charter school operators, ranging from funding issues to internal conflicts to community opposition. However, the four problems listed in the preceding paragraph emerged consistently at the highest percentages across newly created schools, preexisting public schools that converted to charter status, and preexisting private schools that converted to charter status. The operators ranked these problems as "very serious" (2001), and they ranked at over 20 percent of the charter school operators' responses.

Since the responses were divided by category (newly created, preexisting public, and preexisting private), a few facts about these categories are helpful before a description of the responses from the different groups is given. It is interesting to look at relatively old data and then at newer data to see if there have been significant changes. As of the 1998–1999 school year, the fourth-year longitudinal study contained the following information:

- Seventy-two percent of all charter schools were newly created.
- Eighteen percent were preexisting public schools before converting to charter status.
- Ten percent had been preexisting private schools.
- Newly created schools dominated the numbers of charter schools opening each year. (U.S. Department of Education 2001)

WHAT DO NEWER DATA SAY?

This problem clearly is not going away. In a recent study conducted by Policy Analysis for California Education (PACE), a collaborative effort between the University of California, Berkeley, and Stanford University, researchers compared U.S. Census Bureau data with similar data for eighty-four thousand regular public schools. The Census Bureau also surveyed principals from eighty-seven charter schools and 2,847 teachers from those schools during the 1999–2000 school year for the National Center for Educational Statistics (NCES).

They tapped into one particularly disquieting finding: For the most part, charter school operators were not using federal funds to educate disadvantaged children (even though approximately 43 percent were eligible for such assistance), and that could be because principals felt too overwhelmed by the daily pressure of their jobs to complete the requirements for such assistance.

This study has raised controversy because it suggests that many black and Hispanic students, who are attracted to charter schools because of their smaller size and because they offer a stronger sense of community, could be better served in regular public schools. The trade-off is that they could learn with more appreciation in the charter school (if not too hungry to concentrate) but receive better services in the regular public school as a matter of course, not as a hastily arranged afterthought (*Education Week*, April 16, 2003).

The same study found that teachers drawn to charter schools are not fully credentialed, particularly in predominantly black charter schools. Also found was that approximately 48 percent of teachers do not have a teaching license, compared with approximately 9 percent in regular public schools (*Education Week*, April 16, 2003). It is apparent that the same concerns that were listed by the self-reports of their operators in the U.S. Department of Education's fourth-year longitudinal study—although largely favorable to charter schools—show a variety of practical problems (*Education Week*, April 16, 2003).

Student achievement, particularly in the era of the No Child Left Behind (NCLB) legislation, should assume a new focus, according to one of the nation's leading charter school advocates, Chester E. Finn Jr. In a speech Finn gave to charter school operators and authorizers, he warned of disaster if charter school operators did not realize they would be held to the same standards as regular public schools—and should be, in exchange for the freedom from regulation they have enjoyed.

As Finn said:

> [N]ot enough charter schools are doing well enough academically to provide convincing evidence that this is a better educational alternative, especially for poor kids. . . . an awful lot of charter schools are simply not cutting the mustard in terms of academic performance. (Finn 2002, 3)

This concern voiced by a preeminent advocate of school choice and charter schools as a manifestation of that choice should frighten charter school operators and authorizers into paying serious attention to his concerns. Charter schools will soon have to demonstrate that the academic performance of their students meets the standards as set in the NCLB legislation—or go out of business.

LACK OF START-UP FUNDS IS CRITICAL

Problem One: A Lack of Start-up Funds

The first problem, according to an estimated 53.7 percent of newly created charter schools, was a lack of start-up funds. However, this is a sharp contrast to only 26.5 percent of conversion public schools that experienced the same problem. Preexisting private schools that converted to charter status reported a lack of start-up funds at a percentage nearly equal to newly created charter schools (49.4 percent). Large as these percentages may be, they had diminished since the previous survey of charter schools, probably due to infusions of federal funds earmarked for aiding the start-up of charter schools (U.S. Department of Education 2001).

Why would charter schools encounter difficulties with inadequate start-up funds, given the support they experience as a reform? The answer lies in the status of the charter school along with uneven funding formulas for public education. It is significant that more than half of newly created charter schools report a lack of start-up funds, as is the discrepancy between their experience and that of preexisting public schools that converted to charter status. Once a charter is approved by an authorizing agency, monies are made available for the prospective charter school, but sometimes those funds are not accessible at the times that operators need them in order to meet the first payroll and pay other expenses, such as rent (Picus 1998).

And turning again to Finn for an eloquent, heartfelt admonition to charter school operators:

> [C]lean up your schools' acts with respect to budgets, finances, governance and business management. Not just your own schools. All the schools that carry the charter label. We need some self-policing here. The

fastest way to doom this reform movement is to be caught playing fast and loose, or simply ineptly, with public dollars. Weak test scores will kill the charter movement slowly; fiscal shenanigans will kill it fast. (Finn 2002)

OBTAINING FULL FUNDING IN A
TIME OF FISCAL CUTBACKS

In addition, the funding base may not be as high as that of the local public schools. Explanations for discrepancies in funds available to charter schools versus noncharter public schools in the same state can be found in the variety of financing formulas in different states. Charter schools, depending on the legislation in a particular state, may be eligible only for per-pupil monies. Per-pupil allocations are received on an annual basis from school districts, states, or both to cover instructional and non-instructional expenses that range from teacher salaries to textbooks (Finn, Manno, and Vanourek 2000, 12). The per-pupil allocation, whatever it is, also may not cover all the costs of a charter school because charter schools may not receive the total allocation given to noncharter public schools in a particular state (13).

Within states, this contributes to tense relationships and further polarization between charter schools and noncharter public schools. Noncharter public schools may view charter schools as a drain on resources they would normally have if charter school students attended their schools. This situation is currently particularly acute, when states are grappling for resources just for the stark basics to keep their regular public schools afloat.

Headlines about state fiscal cuts and the very real threat of layoff notices for teachers, administrators, and other school staff are rampant as public schools find themselves mired in an economic crisis of gigantic proportions. In New York City, for instance, approximately 3,200 part-time school aides face layoffs. California faces monolithic teacher cuts as well as threats to lower class size, and schools in Oregon have experienced cuts so draconian that their school year was cut by three weeks in 2003. Meanwhile, education interest groups are pointing to the fact that districts are unable to implement the NCLB unless Congress fully funds the recently enacted legislation.

Against this backdrop, two education finance experts, Allan Odden (University of Wisconsin, Madison) and Larry Picus (University of Southern California), were commissioned by Kentucky to perform an analysis of the state's education spending. Odden and Picus concluded that the state is underspending on Pre-K education, and without additional funds applied in a specific formula recommended by the researchers, students cannot be expected to meet state standards.

In fact, Odden and Picus argue that Kentucky should spend an additional $740 million per year to enable each student to reach the state's performance goals. Of this lump sum, the researchers allocate $175 million to expanding existing preschool programs for low-income students, providing all-day kindergarten, reducing class size to fifteen in the elementary grades and twenty-five at the secondary level, offering one-on-one tutoring to students who are falling behind, and increasing the state's allocation of funds to teachers' professional development.

Educators have always said they need more money, but the link between higher spending and increased student achievement has never been made satisfactorily. Now Odden and Picus are trying a new way to make this case, but their approach could spark parent lawsuits against states. This course of action would not be without precedent. Kentucky's funding system was found unconstitutional in 1989 (*Rose v. Council for Better Education*), and the reform package that was enacted by the state legislature had a far-reaching result.

POOR FINANCIAL START CONTRIBUTES TO POOR RELATIONSHIPS

Against this financial backdrop, the "stepchild" relationship charter schools already feel they have with other schools is exacerbated. Charter schools could claim, with some justification, that they are not treated equitably and are left to manage inequitable resources but are expected to produce high student achievement with fewer dollars. As a result, a charter school can open its doors with a variety of strained relationships, both external and internal, since staff may believe they are making professional sacrifices to teach at the charter school. This runs counter to the popular rhetoric of the charter schools movement that places a premium on the fact that everyone wants to be at the charter school. While everyone may like the idea of the charter school, not everyone may be equally pleased about what occurs within its walls.

Private schools that convert to charter school status fall in yet another category. These schools may have converted to charter school status because their funding base was inadequate or shaky, thus making infusions of public funds to support their educational programs highly desirable. Under these circumstances, it is not surprising that nearly half of preexisting private schools would report inadequate start-up funds.

INADEQUATE OPERATING FUNDS POSE
A SIGNIFICANT PROBLEM

Problem Two: Inadequate Operating Funds

In addition to a lack of start-up monies, charter school operators also reported that inadequate operating funds were a barrier (U.S. Department of Education 2001). This information is as current today as it was in 2001. Newly created charter schools (seven out of ten) seem to find this problem most acute (40.4 percent).

Preexisting public schools apparently enjoy more financial security because they have a previous position in, and current link to, the district: only 27 percent report insufficiency of operating funds as a problem. These schools also can benefit from the district's buying size to realize cost reductions, as well as other financial benefits. This percentage, however, remains large enough for some charter schools to obtain the minimum money allowable by law. In return, they are released from many state or district regulations or both.

Certainly, new charter schools can experience financial hardship, particularly at the outset. There are many dramatic anecdotal accounts about the impact that the lack of revenue has on charter school operators. At least a few charter school operators have mortgaged their homes and cashed in their retirement in order to meet the payroll or to cover the initial start-up costs for the school (*Education Week*, December 6, 2000). This demonstrates the unusual, even extreme commitment to the charter school that is a characteristic of most who are active in the charter schools movement. Such dramatic scenarios can be lessened if the school's operators plan a budget that includes the possibility of such situations (Picus 1998).

INADEQUATE PLANNING TIME CAN DEEP-SIX MANY SCHOOLS

Problem Three: Inadequate Planning Time

As with other fledgling reforms, inadequate planning time ranks high as a problem. This is especially severe in newly created charter schools (37.4 percent) and not as acute in preexisting public schools (28 percent) or preexisting private schools (23.9 percent). This suggests that newly created charter schools are pressed with daily management problems, many of which may be unfamiliar to charter school operators, and planning time becomes increasingly difficult to obtain. Everything is new: management, the educational program, the coalition of staff, and the governing board. Relationships have to be forged and nurtured, bonds among staff have to be developed, and a common educational mission should be foremost. Finally, the relationship between staff, parents, students, and the governing board is one of constant negotiation, particularly in the early days.

But other factors contribute to the unfortunate consequence of inadequate planning time. For example, newly created charter schools could try to save money by hiring inexperienced teachers who have dual adjustments: teaching in a charter school and simultaneously beginning a teaching career. This could contribute to a crisis mentality that makes both management and teaching more difficult. In such circumstances, planning time becomes a luxury. (It should be noted that noncharter public schools may resort to the same practice when money is tight.) Or the school's structure could be so loose that reporting lines are blurred and staff members have difficulty identifying those in authority. Yet another possibility is authority that is deliberately diffused among a governing board of parents (who are inexperienced with the daily operation of a school), school staff without management experience, and other educational stakeholders. This diffusion of authority can make daily decision making more difficult as it can be time consuming to reach consensus or to achieve some buy-in from every individual on the governing board.

POOR FACILITIES UNFAIR TO CHARTER CLIENTELE

Problem Four: Inadequate Facilities

Many charter schools report inadequate facilities as a major problem. Newly created charter schools seem to fare the worst, with 35.4 percent reporting problems with their facility. Preexisting public schools have the lowest percentage of problems, but it is still significant: 21.5 percent. This smaller, yet still significant percentage could indicate political problems in a district and relatively low status or priority afforded the charter school, which is consigned to a less desirable building. However, in many if not most cases, it is likely that a converted charter school will remain in the same building that it occupied as a preexisting public school, so perhaps the facility was considered inadequate prior to charter status. Approximately 24.4 percent of preexisting private schools that convert to charter status complain of inadequate facilities, but, again, that most likely was the case prior to charter status, and charter status alone did not create the problem.

Nationally, decaying or otherwise inadequate facilities for public schools have reached the crisis point. According to the National Center for Education Statistics (NCES), in 1999 approximately one-half of U.S. public schools reported that at least one building feature was in less than adequate condition; about four out of ten reported at least one unsatisfactory environmental condition; and close to 10 percent had enrollments that were more than 25 percent greater than the capacity of their permanent buildings. In particular, the plight of inner-city schools has been well documented (Kozol 1991). To a large extent, charter schools can control their size (some states require a minimum enrollment in order to open and operate a charter school). But the large percentage of public schools that report inadequate facilities should be considered to balance charter school operators' reports of inadequate facilities.

DISCUSSION OF CHARTER SCHOOLS'
PROBLEMS AND SOLUTIONS

Possible solutions to some of the top problems confronting charter schools are problematic in themselves, as they highlight the inconsistencies between the ideology of the charter schools movement and how it has played itself out in practice. For example, one answer to inadequate funding for charter schools might be inputs of money from some external source. Charter school operators themselves emphasize the importance of fund-raising from private sources as a part of their jobs. Yet most have little or no background in fund development, and extensive infusions of private monies make charter schools even more of a public/private hybrid.

Additional federal monies are another possibility, but two points are particularly noteworthy. First, during the Clinton administration the federal government continuously increased its financial support of charter schools, expanding funds from $100 million in FY 1999 to $145 million in FY 2000. These funds were provided to states that awarded subgrants to prospective charter school developers and their potential authorizers. These funds can be used for periods of time up to three years, and charter schools with a record of success after three years of operation can be eligible to receive up to 10 percent of their state's total federal grant. Unhappily, these infusions of federal funds did not ease all start-up funding problems (Finn, Manno, and Vanourek 2000).

During the early part of the George W. Bush administration, $30 million was promised to charter schools in 2003, but as can be seen, the NCLB legislation is clearly the priority, not charter schools. The NCLB legislation, after all, has a hidden agenda: to expose the soft underbelly of the regular public schools in all its vulnerability. That is, poorly performing schools will be identified and exposed to public scrutiny; meanwhile, children in these schools will be allowed to leave.

Will there be enough other schools to educate these migrating students? It seems highly unlikely, even if students and families exercise their options and depart. But it also seems more likely that charter schools may shine more brightly, showing what they can do with fewer dollars and fewer students. This is a big opportunity for them, a chance to make good on the promises extended in the NCLB legislation about school choice. If charters end up looking better than regular public schools, they indeed will make good on their original stem-winder rhetoric. They will have shown the rest of the regular public education system how to improve, and they will be the leaders who spearheaded the movement.

At the state level, the chief implication for legislators is that state financing formulas for public schools remain inequitable across states and between noncharter and charter public schools. While public schools in general are afflicted by this inequity, charter schools may suffer an additional penalty if the state legislation does not allocate 100 percent of public school allocations to charter schools (the allowable range can shift from 75 to 100 percent, depending on the state). But again, shrewd charter school operators could seize the opportunity, do some aggressive fund-raising, and outperform regular public schools.

Overall, the lack of monies available for start-up and maintenance of charter schools can be compared to the monies generally available that are earmarked for school improvement or other education reform efforts. According to Robert Slavin (1997), one of the developers of the comprehensive school reform program Success for All, the cost of the reform is the top consideration for building principals and district-level staff who will have to implement it (Lockwood and Secada 1999). These monies, without substantial district commitment over a period of years, can be especially vulnerable to changes in leadership, in school board membership, in personnel shifts at the building site, and in new priorities that crowd forward on a district's agenda. Most commonly, professional development (considered essential for any reform) is likely to be cut or eliminated entirely as districts endure a variety of creative budgeting exercises to cope with their particular financial crises. Almost every constituent has a competing cause for a district to consider, and not everyone's cause can be accommodated.

Generating adequate revenue to sustain a school has been an issue that has plagued charter schools since the first charter school opened in 1991. The charter school that was a preexisting public school tends to fare better financially than the new start-up charter school for reasons that were explained above. However, the conversion charter school may suffer constraints on its mission due to its previous position in a district that the newly created charter school does not have to endure. The most likely scenario for a conversion charter school is that it may be granted charter status by the local school board for political purposes but the level of actual reform or innovation might remain quite limited.

However, newly created schools can see their missions scaled back substantially due to a lack of money. While charter schools cannot charge tuition or fees because they are public schools, they may be forced to operate on a reduced amount of revenue unless they can generate an additional amount from private donors. For this reason, many charter school operators take an entrepreneurial attitude toward public education, fund-raising actively to support their schools, not only to establish them, but to maintain and continue them. Charter school operators who do not anticipate this dimension of their jobs may encounter substantial problems. The majority of charter schools that are forced to cease operation do so because of fiscal problems that range from inexperience and lack of expertise to outright mismanagement (CER 2003). While any public school is a business and legal enterprise, this is markedly the case with charter schools.

The scope of funding and decisions about available funds also affect the vision and mission of charter schools. If a prospective operator, in tandem with prospective board members and staff, has a vision for a school that exceeds available funding streams, that vision must be trimmed in order for the school to be actualized. If a vision is amended, provisions should be made so that staff and prospective parents continue to feel invested in the school, rather than afflicted by the scaling back of mission and goals.

The lack of planning time, however, does not seem particular to charter schools. This issue is cited frequently in the reform literature (Newmann and Associates 1996; Sizer 1984) as a major barrier to realizing any type of innovation or reform. Even highly structured programmatic reforms require professional development and staff discussion time. A particular irony is that when any organization is undergoing change, there is a more pressing need for time to plan and discuss actions that will be taken or that have been taken, along with their consequences. But the process of creating a school or changing to a new way of conducting business as usual can preempt time in the daily schedule that is reserved for planning, unless school leaders make it an absolute. This time for planning is particularly essential if a school is trying to do something in-novative or untried with curriculum and instruction (Lockwood 1997).

A drawback about this independence for newly created charter schools is that they do not have the cushion of the school district to fall back on for a variety of supports. However, an argument can be made that this is part of the charter schools "bargain"—increased deregulation and autonomy for heightened accountability. Charter school advocates typically decry the bureaucracy of the system but note the daily prob-lems without the system's structure that deals with mechanical problems in the school (such as a malfunction of the physical plant). Not being able to hold the central office responsible for such irritants as slow re-sponse time and a lack of supplies also makes the autonomy and ac-countability of the charter school more keenly (sometimes painfully) visible to educational stakeholders.

To deal with the pressures of management and in lieu of the custom-ary support of the district, an increasing number of newly created char-ter schools are choosing an external management company to provide fiscal and leadership expertise. While the number of charter schools managed by private companies may not seem huge, if one looks at the total number of students affected by this turn to private management, the numbers are impressive.

For instance, the largest management company of charter schools is Chancellor Beacon Academies, Inc., which manages seventy-six charter schools with approximately 18,500 students (*Education Week*, May 22, 2002). The next largest, Edison Schools, Inc., manages fifty-three char-ter schools and 21,500 students. And the list goes on.

Another, more limited way in which inexperienced administrators of charter schools deal with the complexities of management is by con-tracting out certain services. This practice is common in schools for such line items as cafeteria services and transportation but can be expanded in schools where administrators are uncomfortable with the manage-ment and direct provision of such services—for a price.

The irony of for-profit management for charter schools is that schools opting for external management seem to be giving up a large part of what drew them originally to the charter school concept. While they have the autonomy to decide how they will be managed, spending a siz-able portion of their budgets on a company that realizes a profit suggests a willingness to abdicate the sought-after autonomy that brought the charter school into being, a need for structure originally provided by the district, and a considerable distrust of the public sector.

Finn scolded the entrepreneurs who have entered the charter school business in a speech he gave to the National Charter School Clearinghouse Conference on September 14, 2002:

> Another malfunction of the charter school machinery is its openness to a small but visible group of greedy school operators more interested in making a few bucks at public expense than running good schools for needy kids. (Finn 2002)

Some of Edison's problems are self-inflicted. But the root of its troubles lies in trying to operate public schools as a successful business. The rules that govern the market—that require companies to establish brand identity, attract capital, and become profitable—contradict essential requirements for creating and maintaining excellent public schools (*Education Week*, August 7, 2002).

Certainly, choosing the private management route does not solve all the problems charter schools have when it comes to managing their services. Given this situation, how many charter schools provide services themselves, and how many choose external sources? According to the same federal report, approximately 36 percent of charter schools provided services themselves. About 34 percent used only an outside provider, and 26 percent used the district as the sole service provider. These findings demonstrate that slightly more than one-third of the operating charter schools provide services themselves while the remainder outsource their services. This indicates that charter schools look at their "autonomy" differently than the rhetoric of the movement suggests. And it leads to the conclusion that the majority of charter schools turn their management over to external providers—including, in many cases, the district from which they converted to charter status.

The problems of management in charter schools show two patterns: opting out through contracts with management companies or considering the school as a personal crusade. Even though other school administrators in the public sector do not have the option of turning their duties over to a different manager, this is a relatively popular option in many charter schools.

In addition, both the Michigan study and the federal longitudinal report on charter schools point to the need for financial leadership and management expertise of skilled and experienced public school administrators. In order for their schools to succeed and in order to deal effectively with their authorizers, charter school operators need backgrounds in school finance and law that they may not possess. Working with different constituent groups and having a tolerance for managing and resolving conflict also would be high on the list of skills that any prospective charter school operator should possess. In addition, these individuals probably will succeed best if they have an impresario's flair for generating positive publicity and additional funds from the private sector. This is an unusual combination of skills and talents for any one individual or small group of individuals to possess. Finally, they would be advised to have expertise in both broad areas of education and specific content areas so that they could hire appropriately, choose curriculum and instructional approaches, and plan an overall educational mission and strategic plan for the school.

Whether those in the charter schools movement value this type of experience and expertise is unclear. Since the movement appears at least in part to be a reaction to the existing public educational system, charter schools have found strength and inspiration in the fact that nontypical individuals often lead them and galvanize individuals around a common mission. These individuals range from parents with no prior educational experience to fully certified administrators who believe in charter schools as the route to positive educational change.

CONCLUSION

By far the most serious problem, from the perspective of the charter schools movement, is the lack of start-up monies and operating funds reported by newly created charter schools. This lack of money for a publicly funded educational alternative highlights financial inequities across the nation in public school spending. However, it also draws attention to a new reform that can argue, with justification, that it is not receiving its slice of the public pie.

If charter legislation does not specify the per-pupil allocation and if charter schools are forced to rely on per-pupil allocations (normally spent on instruction and related costs) to finance their building improvements and leases, at least two things can occur: One, the charter school may be compelled to close before it is tried and tested as an educational alternative, well before the public has an opportunity to be held to any accountability for improved student outcomes. In this scenario, the only accountability is fiscal, and the charter school can argue that it was doomed before it began. This is a particularly pernicious argument and one that plagues several generations of reformers. The plaintive statement, "if only we had the money," is well known in educational circles; it is used to explain substandard programming in a variety of areas, poor teacher morale, and a lack of parental involvement, and, ultimately, it serves as the justification for the failure of a reform. In all financial truth, not everyone's interests can be satisfied through public funds alone.

The second possibility is that the lack of fiscal equity can leave the charter schools movement in a "victim" mode that, although negative, can be very powerful. This situation can help forge tighter, stronger bonds within the movement. The culture of negativity, rather than possibility, is contagious. Excluded from this unity are other, noncharter public schools that face their own financial woes without much public sympathy. (Ask any superintendent of a district that recently failed a referendum.) The lack of fiscal equity also can provide a persuasive argument for lobbyists who try to enact new charter schools legislation or amend current legislation. While charter schools may not achieve fiscal parity with other public schools because of this lobbying, they may net other legislative gains as a part of an overall advantageous political compromise. The source of public funds opens a new source of contention, one that is related closely to the continuing tension between the public and the private that is the peculiarity of charter schools.

While federal funds are hotly contested and prized, unless the prospective charter school operator is truly a proponent of Friedman-like privatization, they can come with a price too high for many charter schools to bear: reporting lines, rules, guidelines, and accountability for how federal dollars are spent. A new public attention is gravitating to public funds for education. In April 2001, the U.S. Department of Education began a massive investigation into what is alleged as the misuse of federal funds spent in support of an investigation during the 1990s (the Clinton administration). This type of federal scrutiny suggests tighter, less permissive days ahead for charter school operators who receive and use federal funds.

Just as inadequate start-up monies and a lack of operating funds can crimp nascent charter schools, the lack of planning time can stunt the development of professional community and abort a well-conceived mission for a school. A culture of continuous refinement, so prized in the current reform literature, cannot be realized when the school day is devoted to a crisis mentality. Many charter schools relate harrowing stories of their beginnings in rough urban neighborhoods and tell heart-warming tales of turnaround success.

Perhaps a more tempered consideration of charter schools is warranted. Although the charter schools movement rejects the notion that it is an alternative to the regular public system, the central concept of school choice is related to creating alternatives to local public schools for students whose parents either cannot afford or are not disposed to sending their children to private schools. The exception occurs in urban environments where a culture of failure—or a public perception of failure—may have permeated neighborhood public schools so thoroughly that parents despair that the school will improve in time to benefit their own children. In these cases, parents may be philosophically inclined to send their children to the neighborhood public school but are afraid their chances of future success will be blighted (Lockwood and Secada 1999).

Charter school advocates are defensive about charter schools that have closed. As of October 2002, the Center for Education Reform (CER), a leading charter school advocacy group, revealed 194 closures, or 6.7 percent of the schools ever given a charter. The center also relates that an additional seventy-seven charter schools "were consolidated back into the school district that originally spawned them for a variety of reasons and are not counted as closures" (CER 2003). It also explains that an additional eighty-four schools received charters but never opened; thus they are not counted as closed.

The leading cause of failure is mismanagement, including fiscal mismanagement. Only one school is cited as closing due to poor academic performance. This calls into question the accountability for student outcomes and the scrutiny the charter school is held to by its authorizer. It also supports the severity of fiscal problems as a leading cause of charter school failure when schools are not mismanaged.

However, advocates of the charter schools movement cloak these failures in rhetoric that suggests only the positive. This rhetoric turns the negative into a positive and is an example of how the charter schools movement may use its problems in ways that will ultimately strengthen it.

Finn summed up the most cogent points about myriad barriers that charter school operators must overcome when he exhorted them in his speech on September 14, 2002, to clean up their way of doing business and focus on the children for whom they were providing an education at public cost:

> The charter movement, by itself, isn't very strong. It also needs legislators, business leaders, media types, philanthropists, higher education figures, civil rights leaders, etc. . . . But public relations won't do the trick if the schools' performance doesn't deserve applause. . . . what finally counts isn't just how many people want something; it's whether that thing is working well. Are the schools succeeding? Are the kids learning? That's our greatest challenge and the one from which we dare not flinch. (Finn 2002)

6

THE SECOND DECADE
OF CHARTER SCHOOLS

Advocates of charter schools frequently talk about the past decade in warlike rhetoric to indicate that they have been through a battle and survived. It is entirely possible that what they viewed as a battle was simply an opening skirmish; the fearsomely tough fights may well lie ahead.

Early in the second decade, the charter schools movement appears poised on a teeter-totter, ready to go either up or down. It is conceivable that charter schools could bounce upward, experiencing continued growth and prosperity. But as likely, they could stall and then experience a drop in popularity, numbers, and enrollments. The history of education in the United States is chock-full of fads and trends that burst onto the scene, enjoyed initial popularity, and then burnt out over time. Charter school advocates need to wonder if their movement is just the latest in the string of such reforms.

Nobody has done a better job chronicling the ups and downs of the charter schools movement than Chester E. Finn Jr., the self-described gadfly of American education. A strong proponent of charter schools, as well as an ongoing booster, Finn nevertheless understands better than most the daunting challenge they face in the second decade. In a speech on September 14, 2002, to the National Charter School Clearinghouse Conference, Finn delivered a blistering description of the current movement:

[T]he national "charter movement" has been leaderless and rudderless, less an army than a loose, messy array of individualistic schools, preoccupied educators and parents, over-eager entrepreneurs, detached analysts and theorists, and advocacy groups that focus intently on their immediate issues but aren't good at helping the broader public understand what charter schools are and why they're a good idea, especially for poor kids. (Finn 2002)

And Finn details what he describes as attacks and sallies on the movement that the movement has *not* overcome skillfully over the past decade:

I sense that some of the wind is going out of the charter sails, the political support for them is weakening a bit, the opposition is stiffening and the problems and criticisms are becoming more apparent than the successes and praise. . . . I don't believe it exaggerates to say that a war is being waged against charter schools. It's a shooting war, a guerilla war and a war of attrition, all at once. (Finn 2002)

Finn feared that the charter schools movement had started to lose its edge. After the first decade, he realized: "The political leaders who grasped the early promise and logic of the charter idea have ridden off into the sunset" (Finn 2002). He recognized that the initial charter school advocates who remain are worn out. Running a school under the best of circumstances is tough work, and running a school without the support of a large central office with its team of curriculum specialists and auditors and grants writers is daunting indeed. But because charter schools receive public monies and operate in the public arena, they have a bevy of rules and regulations to follow. When one considers it was exactly these rules and regulations that drove many of the early zealots to form charter schools, it is understandable that they are wearing down in their efforts to be seen as independent and yet still qualify to quarrel over the public trough.

That the charter school operators labor under the scrutiny of a skeptical and sometimes downright hostile education cartel of state departments of education, universities, and professional educational organizations, particularly teachers' unions, complicates their lives further. Many of these skeptics are quick to call the media's attention to a charter school closure or impropriety. Resulting media articles are then faxed to politicians with a question about the wisdom of continuing this "experiment."

If that was not bad enough, the George W. Bush administration came along and pushed through Congress an intrusive piece of legislation called the No Child Left Behind (NCLB) Act of 2001. The charter school community did its best to ignore this legislation even as it riled the regular public school community. But eventually the U.S. Department of Education got around to charter schools and reminded them that they, too, have to abide by the new rules and regulations. The net of "accountability" that undergirds NCLB was cast wide, and it ensnarled the charter schools along with regular schools. As Finn said in his 2002 speech, charters can ignore the NCLB legislation at their own peril.

THE OPPOSITION OVER THE SECOND DECADE

If Finn is correct in his Cassandra-like predictions, where might charter school operators and authorizers find opposition over the next decade of charter schools that would be sufficient to derail them or to force them into closing their doors? One place seems to be the courthouse.

Teachers' unions, disgusted with the lack of effect they have had in other venues, have begun filing scathing reports (American Federation of Teachers, July 2002) about the condition of charter schools but also have joined in suits questioning their constitutionality—an inventive twist. In Ohio, for example, two years before any legal action was taken, the stirrings of considerable dissent could be seen. A coalition of ten education groups "demanded a moratorium on new charter schools" in the wake of complaints about physical abuse at one charter school and other complaints that a voucher school received payments for students it did not have. These groups demanded that no new schools be opened until increased state oversight was ensured (*Education Week*, January 19, 2000).

State audits revealed a variety of shenanigans at charter schools, including nonexistent textbooks and computers (*Education Week*, January 19, 2000). The opposing organizations included those of the education establishment, such as the Ohio School Boards Association, the Ohio Federation of Teachers, the Ohio PTA, and representatives of school administrators. These complaints and the coalescence of action by state professional groups resulted in promised increased oversight from Ohio's state department and a new "watchdog" mentality—not only from the state, but from the professional associations as well. Once they assumed this new role of outside monitor pressing for improvement, they retained the role.

When Ohio's charter schools were audited, the Ohio state board of education asked the state legislature to reexamine and amend the charter schools law. The department did not withstand outside scrutiny very well when the state auditor wrote that the Ohio Department of Education had not lived up to its responsibility of monitoring the state's ninety-two charter schools. The auditor's recommendation had teeth: "Improve its performance within two months or risk losing oversight" of charter schools entirely (*Education Week*, February 27, 2002). This recommendation, predictably, did get a reaction. The state board of education not only voted unanimously to implement some recommendations that did not "require legislative approval," but it asked a state legislator to "include many of the other recommendations in a bill that he has sponsored to overhaul the charter school system."

CHARTER SCHOOLS SEE COURT CASES UNFOLD IN SECOND DECADE

The Ohio case is illustrative because similar actions could become common in other states once precedent for them has been established. Two years later, the same groups that pressed for increased oversight were back, and this time they filed suit. A court case was brought against charter schools in Ohio, but this suit finally ended up partially dismissed. The plaintiffs had argued that charter schools "violated the state constitution because they are not held to the same standards as regular public schools, usurp citizens' right to govern public schools through a local school board, and are financed by local property taxes" (*Education Week*, April 30, 2003). The plaintiffs, however, included the Ohio School Boards Association and the Ohio Federation of Teachers—the same professional associations that had assumed a watchdog role over charter schools two years earlier.

The judge in the case wrote that charter schools had the right to "create and modify school districts" and that "charter schools are funded only with state dollars," but the rest of the case, which does not question the constitutionality of charter schools in the state, is still pending (*Education Week*, April 30, 2003). The plaintiffs are expected to appeal.

CONTENTION: A TREND FOR CHARTER SCHOOLS?

From the outset, financial management (or mismanagement) has been the bogeyman of the charter schools movement, threatening to burst from a dark closet at any moment and deep-six a school. No one knows this better than Finn, who warned charter school advocates in his 2002 speech that they needed to clean up their act where finances were concerned. Finn reminded the operators that nothing would kill a charter school more quickly than financial mismanagement or the appearance of mismanagement, the most common reason charter schools are forced to shut down (Finn 2002).

Finn mentioned other ways the charter schools movement might kill itself. He indicted "feckless" authorizers who issue charters far too casually and are unwilling to undertake any oversight (Finn 2002). All too often, as has been noted by their critics, authorizers appear much more comfortable being boosters than regulators. As such, they champion charter schools much more than they monitor them. This should change with the new Regulations for Charter School Authorizers for Title I Funds, released from the U.S. Department of Education in March 2003. These federally mandated regulations, which stem from NCLB legislation, impose a federally mandated burden on previously free charter school authorizers. They either regulate their charges or run the risk that their schools will be turned over to less-friendly departments of education for oversight.

Another way that charter schools could flounder, suggested Finn, would be if they succumbed to their own ego needs and refused to bond with others in a true "movement" (Finn 2002). The Washington insider said charter schools needed to come together to lobby effectively for the movement instead of quarreling among themselves over turf and territory. For the first decade, the charter schools and their allies operated as a loose collection of groups and organizations. If they are to prosper in the second decade, they will need to heed Finn's recommendations and begin to gather media support, conduct persuasive public relations, attract shrewd entrepreneurs, and enlist others to join the charter bandwagon.

That challenge, given the nature of charter school operators and parents, may be difficult to achieve. But without such an effort, the movement might not be properly prepared for the struggles ahead. One thing is clear: charter school critics are not going to go away, particularly when the public dollars for support of schools—charter and regular schools alike—remain scarce. In addition, the NCLB Act forces accountability of the regular schools, the likes of which they have never experienced before. Misery loves company, and it is highly likely that the public school crowd will say loudly: "What about accountability for charter schools—they're publicly funded too."

ANOTHER VIEW OF CHARTER SCHOOLS
FOR THE SECOND DECADE

When charter schools are discussed, the topic almost always focuses exclusively on newly formed charters, those started by folks who for a variety of reasons found the regular schools wanting. But the regular school districts are allowed to form charters too, and several have. These schools tend to remain strongly tied to their host districts and as such remain aloof from the start-up charters. The gap between them is such that some charter school advocates refer to the converted public school charters as "copy charters" and not the real thing. That description is probably accurate.

But in the second decade, these so-called copy charters might increase in number and popularity. Even in the first decade, a few lone voices, such as Joe Schneider, then the deputy executive director of the American Association of School Administrators (AASA), were advising superintendents to consider forming their own charters within their districts (Conversation with author, 2003).

Schneider's basic argument is that a charter created by a local school board that operates within the district structure has the advantages of newness, innovation, and flexibility, and yet it retains all the protections of the district bureaucracy. Schneider said a superintendent faced with parents who wanted small class sizes, greater parental involvement, specialized programs, and "freedom" could provide those things within the district so that parents would not have to pull their children out and enroll them elsewhere. The obvious advantage to the district is that it retains the funds. Other advantages would accrue to the superintendent, Schneider suggested. He or she could appear progressive, innovative, and competitive.

Not a whole lot of districts took Schneider up on his suggestion. But that could change with the implementation of the NCLB Act. School districts now have to provide parents who have children in schools that are found wanting with an alternative place for them to be educated. If precedent means anything, these parents will find the options to be limited to schools that look much like the ones they want to leave. It stands to reason that many of these parents will want to enroll their children in a charter school that can make the claim for the things parents want, beginning with small class size and personal attention to their children. A well-informed superintendent might well designate one or more of her schools as charters to retain the students. Such schools might also find it easier than regular schools in the district to recruit and retain the quality staff that the NCLB law provides.

This co-opting of charter schools could indeed be a brilliant stroke, if school administrators heed Schneider's admonition to provide parents with alternatives within their own districts. More than just a safety valve, conversion charters, when conceived of in this new sense, could be interesting and worthwhile schools. They could actually address the needs of all their pupils, raise achievement scores, please parents, attract quality educators, and, in the process, make the superintendent and the school board appear responsive.

Maybe conversion charters could become the darlings of the second decade of charters. Whereas little evidence exists to suggest charter schools in the first decade influenced public schools even a little bit, conversion charters that operate as an essential part of the other schools in the district might well be an exception. Freed up from bureaucratic rules and regulations that thwart innovation in other schools, the charter schools might well point out what can be accomplished when they have increased autonomy. Today most charter principals are excluded from seminars, conventions, and gatherings of public school principals. That scenario is not likely for charter school principals who operate within the district. They will remain members of the district administrative team and have access to the same services as their counterparts.

The district would manage the charter schools' books, route their buses, feed their students, and enroll their personnel into retirement systems. The teachers in the district's charter schools would be eligible for the same professional development opportunities as all the other district teachers. In return, the charter schools would operate as "lighthouse" schools in which parents could find an alternative educational setting for their children without being forced to leave the community's public school system. It would be ironic—but not totally implausible—in this second decade of charters for conversion charter schools to emerge as the movement's salvation.

REFERENCES

American Federation of Teachers. July 2002. Do charter schools measure up? The charter school experiment after 10 years. Washington, D.C.: Author.

Center for Education Reform (CER). http://edreform.com/, 2003 [accessed July 6, 2003].

Cremin, L. A. 1964. *The transformation of the school: Progressivism in American education, 1876–1957*. New York: Knopf.

Doyle, D., L. V. Gerstner Jr., W. B. Johnston, and R. D. Semerad. 1994. *Reinventing education: Entrepreneurship in America's public schools*. New York: Dutton.

Education Commission of the States (ECS). Charter schools. www.ecs.org, April 2003 [accessed July 10, 2003].

Education Week. January 19, 2000. More oversight sought for Ohio school choice. www.edweek.org [accessed July 6, 2003].

Education Week. December 6, 2000. No rest for leaders of charter schools. www.edweek.org [accessed July 6, 2003].

Education Week. February 27, 2002. Audit spurs drive to revamp Ohio's charter schools system. www.edweek.org [accessed July 6, 2003].

Education Week. May 22, 2002. Edison reels amid flurry of bad news. www.edweek.org [accessed July 6, 2003].

Education Week. August 7, 2002. Heidi Steffens and Peter W. Cookson Jr. Limitations of the market model. www.edweek.org/ew/newstory.cfm?slug=43steffens.h21 [accessed July 5, 2003].

Education Week. December 11, 2002. Ohio poised to reorganize charter school oversight. www.edweek.org [accessed July 6, 2003].

Education Week. January 15, 2003. www.edweek.org [accessed July 6, 2003].

Education Week. April 16, 2003. Charter schools found lacking resources. www.edweek.org [accessed July 6, 2003].

Education Week. April 30, 2003. California charter-funding fight hits home. www.edweek.org [accessed July 6, 2003].

Finn, C. E., Jr. 2002. The war on charter schools. Speech presented at conference. National Charter School Clearinghouse Conference, September 14. www.ncsc.info/newsletter/conference/keynote.htm [accessed July 6, 2003].

Finn, C. E. Jr., B. V. Manno, and G. Vanourek. 2000. *Charter schools in action: Renewing public education.* Princeton, N.J.: Princeton University Press.

Friedman, M. 1955. The role of government in education. www.school-choices.org/ [accessed July 6, 2003].

Hill, P. T. 2000. How home-schooling will change public education. *Hoover Digest,* no. 2.

Kanstoroom, M., and C. E. Finn Jr. 1999. Overview: Thirty-four years of dashed hopes. In *New directions: Federal education policy in the twenty-first century,* edited by C. E. Finn Jr., M. Kanstoroom, and M. Petrilli. Washington, D.C.: Thomas B. Fordham Foundation.

Kozol, J. 1991. *Savage inequalities: Children in America's schools.* New York: Crown.

Lasch, C. 1978. *The culture of narcissism: American life in an age of diminishing expectations.* New York: Norton.

Lieberman, M. 1989. *Privatization and educational choice.* New York: St. Martin's Press.

Lockwood, A. T. 1997. *Conversations with educational leaders: Contemporary viewpoints on education in America.* Albany: State University of New York Press.

Lockwood, A. T., and W. S. Secada. 1999. *Transforming education for Hispanic youth: Exemplary practices, programs, and schools.* Washington, D.C.: National Clearinghouse on Bilingual Education, Center for the Study of Language and Education, Graduate School of Education & Human Development, George Washington University.

Nathan, J. 1999. *Charter schools: Creating hope and opportunity for American education.* San Francisco, Calif.: Jossey-Bass.

National Commission on Excellence in Education. 1983. *A nation at risk: The imperative for educational reform.* Washington, D.C.: U.S. Department of Education.

Newmann, F. M., and Associates. 1996. *Authentic achievement: Restructuring schools for intellectual quality*. San Francisco, Calif.: Jossey-Bass.

Oakes, J. 1985. *Keeping track: How schools structure inequality*. New Haven, Conn.: Yale University Press.

Picus, L. 1998. Management issues [in charter schools]. Madison: Wisconsin Center for Education Research (unpublished manuscript).

Ravitch, D. 2000. *Left back: A century of failed school reforms*. New York: Simon & Schuster.

Secretary's Commission on Achieving Necessary Skills (SCANS). 1991. Report for the U.S. Department of Labor. Washington, D.C.: GPO.

Sizer, T. R. 1984. *Horace's compromise: The dilemma of the America high school*. Boston: Houghton Mifflin.

Slavin, R. E. 1997. *Every child, every school: Success for all*. Thousand Oaks, Calif.: Corwin Press.

Third International Mathematics and Science Study (TIMSS). 1995. Washington, D.C.: National Center for Education Statistics.

Tyack, D. B. 1974. *The one best system: A history of American urban education*. Cambridge: Harvard University Press.

U.S. Department of Education. 1998. *Goals 2000: Reforming education to improve student achievement*. Washington, D.C.: Author.

U.S. Department of Education. 2001. *National study of charter schools: Fourth year report*. Washington, D.C.: Author.

U.S. Department of Education. The impact of the new Title I regulations on charter schools: Non-regulatory guidance. www.uscharterschools.org/pdf/fr/nclb_guidance.pdf, 2003 [accessed August 8, 2003].

Wells, A. S., with L. Artiles, S. Carnochan, C. W. Cooper, C. Grutzik, J. J. Holme, A. Lopez, J. Scott, J. Slayton, and A. Vasudeva. 1998. *Beyond the rhetoric of charter school reform: A study of ten California school districts* [UCLA Charter School Study]. Los Angeles: University of California.

INDEX

ABOUT THE AUTHOR

Anne Turnbaugh Lockwood is an educational policy analyst based in Washington, D.C., where she was an issues analysis director at the American Association of School Administrators from 2001–2003. She is the author of over one hundred articles on education as well as numerous educational reports, monographs, and four books: *Tracking: Conflicts and Resolutions*; *Character Education: Controversy and Consensus*; *Conversations with Educational Leaders: Contemporary Viewpoints on Education in America;* and *Standards: From Policy to Practice*. As a policy analyst and writer, Lockwood was active in a host of special projects sponsored by the North Central Regional Educational Laboratory and the U.S. Department of Education.

At the University of Wisconsin, Madison, she initiated and directed two nationally respected publications programs for the National Center on Effective Secondary Schools (1986–1990) and the National Center on Effective Schools (1990–1994). She is a former honorary fellow in both the Department of Curriculum and Instruction and the Wisconsin Center for Education Research at the University of Wisconsin, Madison. Lockwood is the recipient of the 1993 American Educational Research Association Interpretive Scholarship Award for relating research to practice and the Distinguished Achievement Award of the School of Education, University of Wisconsin, Madison. She holds a Ph.D. in educational psychology from the University of Illinois at Urbana–Champaign.